CUT UP THIS BOOK!

Special Occasions

CUT UP THIS BOOK!

Special Occasions

Emily Hogarth

Running Press
PHILADELPHIA · LONDON

A QUARTO BOOK

Copyright © 2013 Quarto Inc.
Published by Running Press,
A Member of the Perseus Books Group

Color separation in Hong Kong by Modern Age
Repro House Ltd

Printed in China by 1010 Printing International

Books published by Running Press are available
at special discounts for bulk purchases in the
United States by corporations, institutions, and
other organizations. For more information,
please contact the Special Markets
Department at the Perseus Books Group, 2300
Chestnut Street, Suite 200, Philadelphia, PA
19103, or call (800) 810-4145, ext. 5000, or
e-mail special.markets@perseusbooks.com.

ISBN: 978-0-7624-4787-9

Library of Congress Control Number:
2012917975

9 8 7 6 5 4 3 2

Digit on the right indicates the number of
this printing

Conceived, designed, and produced by
Quarto Publishing plc
The Old Brewery
6 Blundell Street
London N7 9BH

QUAR: CUHH

Project editor Lily de Gatacre
Art editor Joanna Bettles
Art director Caroline Guest
Design assistant Nadine Resch
Copy editor Sarah Hoggett
Proofreader Chloe Todd Fordham
Indexer Ann Barrett
Photography Phil Wilkins
Project photography Nicki Dowey

Creative director Moira Clinch
Publisher Paul Carslake

Running Press Book Publishers
2300 Chestnut Street
Philadelphia, PA 19103-4371

Visit us on the web!
www.runningpress.com

CONTENTS

PROJECTS

Getting started (pages 12–35)

The first section will introduce you to the key techniques needed to start papercutting. You will find out how to pick the right paper, master your craft knife, use templates, and design your own papercuts to fit your special occasion.

Cutting methods are demonstrated in photographs so you can compare and check your technique.

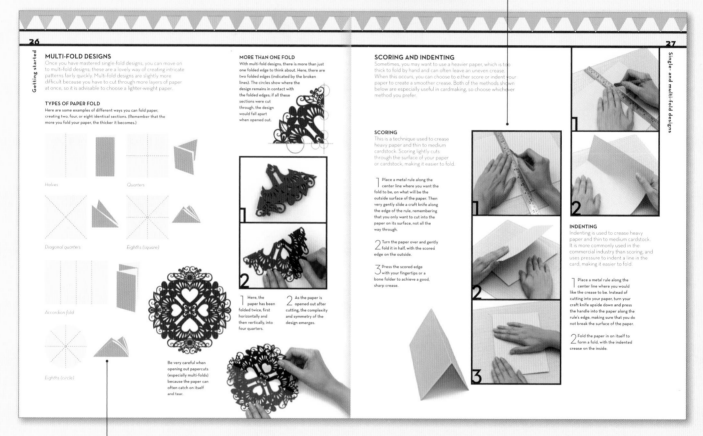

Diagrams clearly illustrate important points, key skills, and explain common pitfalls.

26

Getting started

MULTI-FOLD DESIGNS

Once you have mastered single-fold designs, you can move on to multi-fold designs, these are a lovely way of creating intricate patterns fairly quickly. Multi-fold designs are slightly more difficult because you have to cut through more layers of paper at once, so it is advisable to choose a lighter-weight paper.

TYPES OF PAPER FOLD

Here are some examples of different ways you can fold paper, creating two, four, or eight identical sections. (Remember that the more you fold your paper, the thicker it becomes.)

Halves

Quarters

Diagonal quarters

Eighths (square)

Accordion fold

Eighths (circle)

MORE THAN ONE FOLD

With multi-fold designs, there is more than just one folded edge to think about. Here, there are two folded edges (indicated by the broken lines). The circles show where the design remains in contact with the folded edges; if all these sections were cut through, the design would fall apart when opened out.

1 Here, the paper has been folded twice, first horizontally and then vertically, into four quarters.

2 As the paper is opened out after cutting, the complexity and symmetry of the design emerges.

Be very careful when opening out papercuts (especially multi-folds) because the paper can often catch on itself and tear.

SCORING AND INDENTING

Sometimes, you may want to use a heavier paper, which is too thick to fold by hand and can often leave an uneven crease. When this occurs, you can choose to either score or indent your paper to create a smoother crease. Both of the methods shown below are especially useful in cardmaking, so choose whichever method you prefer.

SCORING

This is a technique used to crease heavy paper and thin to medium cardstock. Scoring lightly cuts through the surface of your paper or cardstock, making it easier to fold.

1 Place a metal rule along the center line where you want the fold to be, on what will be the outside surface of the paper. Then very gently slide a craft knife along the edge of the rule, remembering that you only want to cut into the paper on its surface, not all the way through.

2 Turn the paper over and gently fold it in half, with the scored edge on the outside.

3 Press the scored edge with your fingertips or a bone folder to achieve a good, sharp crease.

INDENTING

Indenting is used to crease heavy paper and thin to medium cardstock. It is more commonly used in the commercial industry than scoring, and uses pressure to indent a line in the card, making it easier to fold.

1 Place a metal rule along the center line where you would like the crease to be. Instead of cutting into your paper, turn your craft knife upside down and press the handle into the paper along the rule's edge, making sure that you do not break the surface of the paper.

2 Fold the paper in on itself to form a fold, with the indented crease on the inside.

27

Single- and multi-fold designs

Easily find the right template for this project at the back of the book.

Follow the step-by-steps for great results.

The skill level symbol points to the difficulty of the project—level 1, 2, or 3.

Projects
(pages 36–91)
Twenty five fantastic and varied projects to follow so you can hone your skills while creating original pieces of art which will give your special occasions a personal touch.

A graphic at the beginning of each project will point out the trickiest areas to cut. Take extra care around these areas.

Using a craft knife or a pair of scissors, cut along this line to cut the page straight out of the book.

Each template links to a project with similar techniques so you can follow the steps and keep on the right track.

Templates
(pages 92–142)
At the back of the book you will find 60 unique templates that you can cut out from the book or photocopy to use again and again.

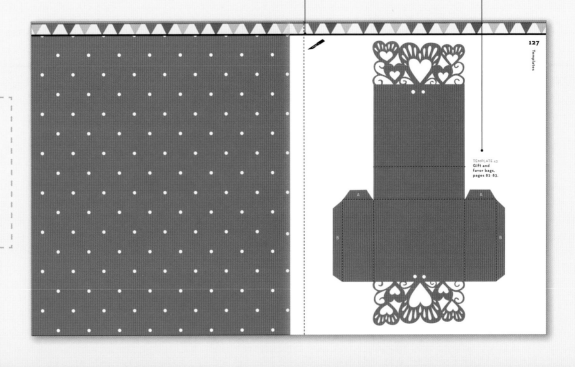

TEMPLATE 43
Gift and favor bags,
pages 82–85.

I love papercutting! There, I've said it. I love that something as simple as a piece of paper can be magically transformed into something of beauty and something to be treasured.

I was introduced to papercutting while studying Textile Design at Edinburgh College of Art. It was a tool for me to create large stencils to screen-print my designs onto fabric. During my studies, I developed my own papercutting style and began to create papercuts that were more than just stencils; they became artworks in their own right. I found that I could create something magical and delicate out of a single piece of paper, changing it from an everyday essential to something of beauty. After Art College I worked with some greetings card companies as a freelance designer, and learned to translate my designs onto lots of different products. I also started taking on commissions for people for wedding gifts or birthdays, and started to build up my reputation as a papercutting designer.

For me, papercutting is a way of drawing, and I use my craft knife like most illustrators would use a pencil. I love the clean, sharp lines you get from papercutting—it is a very old craft and yet can look so fresh, graphic, and bold today.

I am inspired by a wide variety of things, from Scandinavian architecture, to beautiful stationery. My rule is, if it makes me smile then it's worth having around. I believe that inspiration can be found in almost anything—all you have to do is look. I love collecting design and illustration books and have a nice collection now that I can always go to when in need of some inspiration. Websites and blogs are a great way to see what is going on in the design world and I can often get lost for hours browsing beautiful designs from around the world. I also love having lots of objects and images around me, and am a bit of a hoarder of lovely illustrations and designs (sometimes to my husband's annoyance as they can take up a lot of room!). I find great inspiration in other artists and designers too; I think their passion and dedication to their own crafts often inspires me to develop my own work more.

I am lucky enough to have my own studio away from my home that I go to every day with my little West Highland Terrier, Mary—it's where all the magic takes place. I love going to my studio and starting a new project, looking through all my books and on the Internet for ideas, and then translating them into new designs. I particularly love creating personal papercut commissions for individuals. I love the intimacy that you can include and the subtle details that can mean so much to the recipient— the name of a loved one, or an important date hidden in the petal of a flower. I enjoy combining these personal details with my own designs to create a work of art for someone to treasure.

Today, I am busy creating new stationery ranges of my own, as well as developing some commercial designs. Working with commercial companies is a great way to get papercut designs out into the market and adds a little magic to everyday packaging and products.

For this book, I wanted to create papercut projects that can be used for lots of different parties and special occasions throughout the year and add a lovely personal element to your events. I hope that you will find these projects inspiring and find the confidence to go away and start creating your own designs. Enjoy, have fun, and have a beautifully decorated party! Happy cutting!

Emily x

1
GETTING STARTED

TOOLS AND MATERIALS

One of the great things about papercutting is that all you really need to get started is a piece of paper and a cutting implement—although, over the years, a few extra tools have been designed to make the craft easier. This section sets out the essentials.

ESSENTIAL TOOLS

All the projects in this book have been designed to be made with as few tools as possible, but there is a basic recommended list of equipment that you should have, which is shown below. The following pages go into more detail about how to choose your paper, scissors, and craft knife, and set out some basic cutting and folding techniques.

Paper

It is a good idea to have a wide variety of papers (1) available, so that you have them to hand when you need to use them. For information about what papers are best for papercutting, see page 19.

Cardstock

As with paper, it is a good idea to have different weights of cardstock (2) to hand for different projects.

Tracing vellum/carbon paper

Using tracing vellum is a great way to transfer an image to another piece of paper; carbon paper (3) is also used for this purpose. See page 24 for instructions on how to use them.

Pencil

A pencil (4) and a pencil sharpener are essential in any tool kit for drawing or modifying your designs. A medium-grade pencil such as a #2 is recommended, as it gives a crisp, fine line and can still be easily erased.

Eraser

Use an eraser (5) to get rid of any unwanted pencil marks on your final piece. Although slightly more expensive, a kneaded eraser (6) is particularly effective for this.

Adhesives

There are many forms of adhesives on the market. Spray adhesives (7, over the page) are a good option for papercutting, because they have less moisture in them and therefore will not warp your paper. It is easy to get an even coverage without the risk of the adhesive seeping onto the right (visible) side. These should always be used in a well-ventilated area.

Double-sided tape (8) is a useful alternative and is less messy than conventional glues. This comes in rolls with two sticky sides. Peel off the backing paper from one side and place that side of the tape on your paper, then remove the backing paper on the other side of the tape so that you can attach it to another surface.

Glue sticks (9) and glue pens (10, over the page) are great because you only need a few small dots of glue on the back of your artwork to secure it in place.

When using water-based craft glue or other liquid glues, do not put too much on your papercut: you don't want your artwork to get damp, since this will warp and ruin the finished design. To raise paper or cardstock slightly off the surface and give a three-dimensional effect, try foam sticky pads or glue dots. This is a great method to use on greetings cards and gift tags (see pages 80–81).

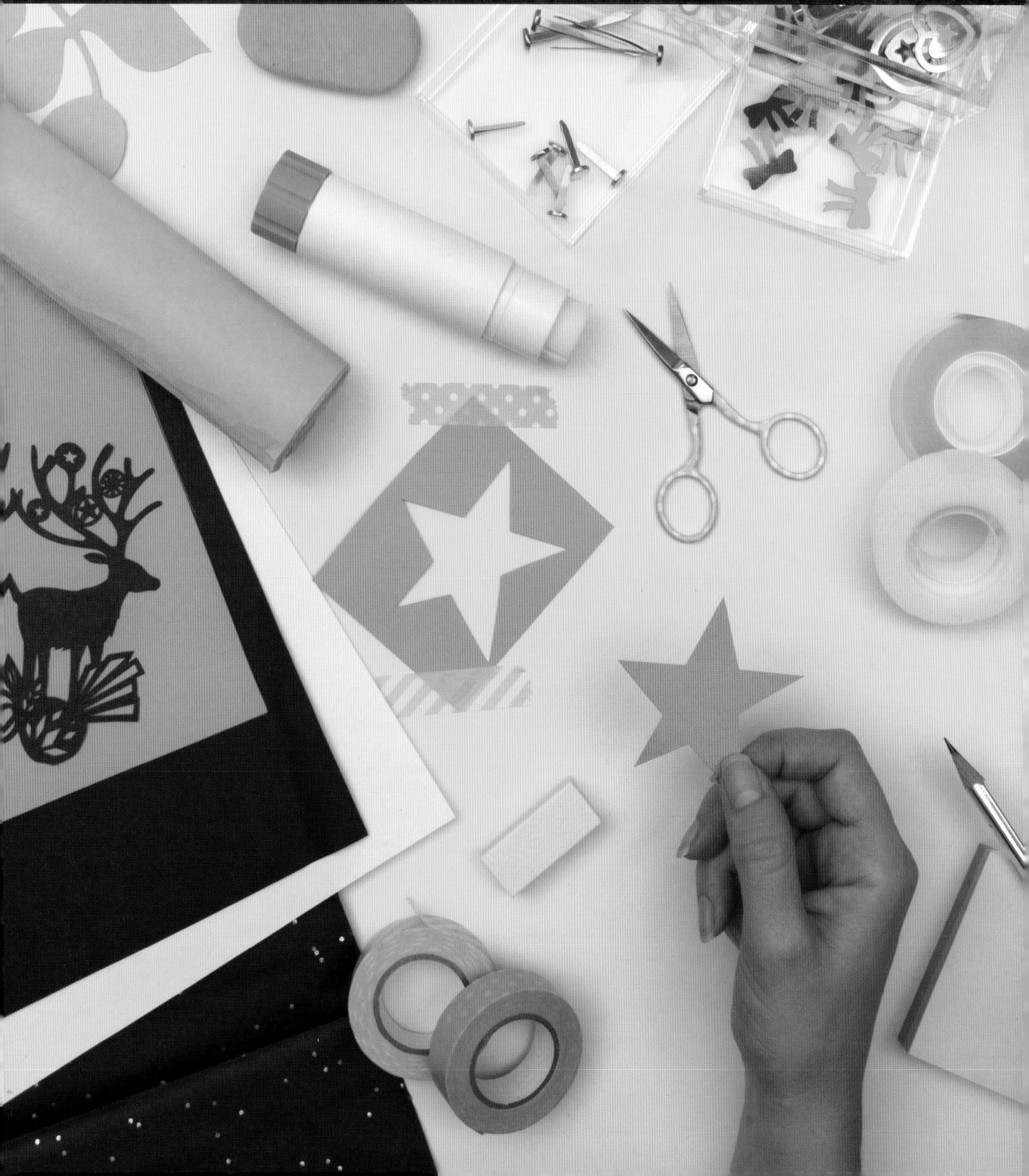

Low-tack tape

You will need a good low-tack tape for securing your template to your chosen paper so that it does not move as you are cutting. Invisible tape (11, previous page) is best for this sort of work, since it can easily be removed from the paper without ruining your papercut. I always recommend testing the tape on a scrap piece of paper first before you begin a project, so that you know that you can remove it afterward.

Scissors

Scissors (12, previous page) are traditionally used for papercutting and there is a huge range available, some of which can be re-sharpened when the blades become dull. Be sure to buy a pair that fits comfortably in your hand, with small, sharp tips for cutting small areas. It is worth investing in a good-quality pair of scissors, but you can start with a small pair of simple embroidery scissors.

Craft knife

A hand-held knife with replaceable blades (13) is perfect for creating accurate, neat, and intricate cuts. This tool is needed for almost all the projects in this book and can be purchased from most craft/art stores. Always have new blades to hand, since blades need to be changed regularly to make clean cuts.

Metal rule

Always use a metal rule (14) when cutting straight edges with a craft knife, since the knife can slip and cut into plastic and wooden rules.

Cutting mat

A self-healing cutting mat (15) protects your table top and prevents your craft knife from slipping and you cutting yourself. Cutting mats can be purchased in different sizes and they usually have a ruled grid on them, which is helpful in lining edges up.

USEFUL EXTRAS

The following items are not essential, but good to have to hand.

Bone folder

Made from plastic not real bone, this tool helps you to create smooth, crisp creases and folds. Bone folders (16) are readily available from craft stores.

Sewing tools

A sewing machine is a great way to secure pieces of paper together (see pages 54–55), a needle (17) can be used to pierce small holes in your artwork, and threads (18) are great to hang projects such as garlands.

Sketchbook

Inspiration could strike you at any time, so keep a sketchbook (19) that you can easily carry around, colored pencils, and fiber-tip pens to ensure that you never miss an opportunity to jot down an idea.

Ribbon

This is another useful material that's great to have in your tool kit to finish off cards and tags. Often, small scraps of ribbon (20) are all that you need, so save up remnants from gift wrappings or sewing projects.

Brass paper fasteners

These (21, previous page) are a great way of adding hinged, moving parts to your projects.

Wooden sticks

Keep wooden skewers (22) and toothpicks (23) in your craft box as they can be utilized for a number of projects such as cake toppers or food flags.

Pins and clips

Household staples such as pins (24), thumbtacks (25), and paperclips can come in handy for a multitude of tasks: keeping papers together, attaching inspiring images to your pinboard, or holding paper securely while glue dries. It is a good idea to keep some nearby.

Tool kits

Remember to read the instructions and tool kit for each project in this book before you begin. Sometimes extra equipment, such as tealights, hair bands, or a drinking straw may be required or recommended.

Paper is the key component for papercutting: from a single piece, you can create a beautiful, delicate, and treasured artwork. Before you begin any project, therefore, it is essential that you think carefully about what paper you are going to use.

HISTORY OF PAPERCUTTING

Paper was originally created as a material to document, write, and illustrate onto. Over the years, attention has turned to the material itself and the art of papercutting has allowed paper to become the object of art, not just the medium for other art forms.

Paper was first created in China in the 1st century CE. Because there was such skill involved in the process of producing paper, an aesthetic appreciation for the material itself developed and paper began to be used as the object of art forms. Origami (the art of folding paper) and papercutting are examples of this—art forms that allow the material to be the main object. Although in the beginning it was only available to the wealthy and royal, over time it developed into a form of folk art, being embraced by those who couldn't afford expensive tools and materials such as paints, canvases, and brushes.

In the West, it took longer for paper to become more than just a medium to write or illustrate on. Papercutting moved west through Asia and into the Middle East, and by the 16th century it had reached Europe. Along the way, different countries and cultures developed their own interpretations and styles. These interpretations have left us with a diverse and rich range of papercutting history to look back on.

In Poland, the tradition is known as *wycinanki*, which translates as "cut out." Papercuts were used to decorate homes, especially around festive holidays such as Easter and Christmas. The Polish papercutting style uses bright-colored papers in layers and usually depicts rural or folk scenes and motifs such as roosters. In Germany and Switzerland, papercutting is called *Scherenschnitte*, which translates as "scissor cuts." This style of cutting uses small embroidery-style scissors and is often a folded design. The Danish storyteller Hans Christian Andersen accompanied some of his tales with simple folded and cut illustrations similar to *Scherenschnitte* designs and *Scherenschnitte* is still a strong folk tradition in these countries today.

Around the 18th century, the art of paper-cut silhouettes became very popular as a way of recording family portraits. Cheaper than commissioning a painted portrait, these silhouettes—or cameos, as they sometimes were called—became very fashionable, especially in England, France, and Germany. It was also around this time that the Mexican form of papercutting known as *papel picado* started to develop. Unlike the European papercutting methods, where scissors or knives were used, Mexicans used chisels to create their decorations out of tissue paper, chiseling up to 40 banners at a time. These Mexican banners are commonly used to decorate towns and homes around religious holidays and have been closely associated with the Day of the Dead holiday.

Recently, papercutting has seen a revival and is becoming more popular among artists and crafters alike. Many of today's artists are influenced by its history and traditions, and it can be seen in movies, design, fashion, and art all over the globe. Modern artists continue to breathe new life into this art form and push it forward, while still retaining the traditional key elements—paper, a cutting tool, and their imagination.

CHOOSING PAPER

Any paper can be used in papercutting, but some types are definitely better than others. You will also find that certain papers are not as suitable for certain projects as others. With experience, you will discover which types of paper work best for you and for the style of papercut that you are creating.

Paper weights

It's a good idea to try out different thicknesses (especially in the beginning), so that you know what these different weights actually feel like in your hands. So long as you know what thickness you like and need for a particular type of design, you'll know what to buy. Paper is described in different ways, but the most common description is by weight. This differs in the United States and Europe.

In the United States, paper weight is measured in pounds per ream. A ream is usually 500 sheets—so the heavier the ream, the thicker the paper. For example, printer paper is roughly 100 lb per ream, while artists' drawing paper is roughly 220 lb per ream.

In the United Kingdom and other countries outside of the United States, paper is measured in grams per square meter (gsm). Printer paper is roughly 80 gsm, while artists' drawing paper is roughly 150 gsm.

Keep in mind that heavier-weight papers are more suitable for flat, open papercutting. A papercut with fine details would be extremely difficult to cut out of a heavyweight cardstock. Cardstock is also not ideal for any project in which you would attempt to cut multiple layers at once. On the other hand, lighter-weight papers are better for folded designs or intricate designs, but would not be a good choice for anything that needs to be strong or stand upright, such as greetings cards. Consider using multiple paper weights within a single project, for example, create an intricate papercut using lightweight paper and attach to the front of a greetings card constructed from heavy cardstock.

Paper quality

A good rule of thumb is the higher the quality of your paper, the better. However, it's a good idea to play around with different types, since this allows you to find out what works best for you and for different projects.

High-quality, acid-free paper is always a really good option; it is the preferred choice of most papercutters because it cuts cleanly, is a good thickness, doesn't fade over time, and comes in a huge variety of colors.

Some papers, such as recycled papers are made up of lots of short fibers, which means they are more likely to tear when being cut and are therefore not an ideal choice for papercutting (although they can be used as backing papers).

Design considerations

When choosing the paper for a project, you will also need to consider the color and pattern of the paper. This may be to fit in with a particular theme, occasion, or color-scheme—you can find more information on this on pages 32–33. A single-colored paper will show off the intricate detail of a papercut, while a patterened paper might distract from a delicate design. When designing something that will be visible from both sides, make sure that the paper is colored on both sides. If you want a specific color of paper and you can't find it, consider doing your design on white paper and then spray painting it in your chosen color.

Alternative choices

Other types of paper that are not often used in traditional papercutting are crêpe paper and tissue paper. Crêpe paper is a form of tissue paper that has been treated to create tiny gatherings over the paper's surface, which creates the unusual texture. Tissue paper is one of the thinnest forms of paper, which makes it very fragile for cutting. In Mexico, however, tissue paper is used to create bright, paper-cut bunting known as *papel picado*—so although there are guidelines to what paper to choose, there is no right or wrong. Crêpe and tissue papers can add a different dimension to your projects so give them a go.

CUTTING WITH A CRAFT KNIFE

A craft knife or X-acto knife is a popular choice of cutting tool with papercutters, because it can give you very fine detail and is easy to use—but there are some things to remember when starting out.

When choosing your craft knife there are a few things to consider. It is really important that you use a knife that has replaceable blades or a blade that you can sharpen; your blade must be sharp at all times. Having a sharp blade not only means that your cuts will be cleaner and smoother, but it is also safer since the blade is less likely to slip and cut you.

Change the blade when you feel your craft knife dragging slightly in the paper; this will become easier to spot the more you practice. Also check the point of your blade regularly, because as soon as it has been blunted or damaged it may tear your paper and ruin all your hard work.

Another thing to consider when choosing your craft knife is the handle. There are lots of different types available, from flat and long, to circular and short. Most papercutters will find a knife that they particularly like and stick with it. In the beginning, it is worth trying a few different varieties to find out what feels most comfortable and works best for you.

Always use a self-healing cutting mat when cutting with a craft knife. These are easily available in art and craft stores and come in a variety of sizes. A cutting mat not only protects your work surface and keeps the blade from blunting too quickly, it also stops the blade from slipping, thus preventing any accidents. Other materials such as board can be used, but self-healing cutting mats are definitely the safest and most practical solution.

Watch your cutting
Overcutting and undercutting are the terms used when you cut either too far (below right) or not far enough (below left). Try to be as accurate as you possibly can—but if you do overcut or undercut, don't worry too much: it's all part of the learning process.

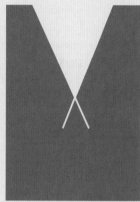

Safety first
- Always keep blades in a safe place—even used ones, which are still exceedingly sharp. An old preserves jar (with its lid) is the ideal place to store them safely.
- Be sure to always store your knife with the blade tip covered and facing downward, to avoid any accidents.

CHANGING BLADES

It is important to change your blade regularly, since a blade that is not sharp will drag, rather than cut, through your paper. As a general rule, I recommend using a new blade for each project. Always read the instructions on any craft knife that you buy carefully, because each make and style will vary slightly. A safe method for changing the blades on a surgical scalpel (which was used to make all the projects in this book) is demonstrated at right.

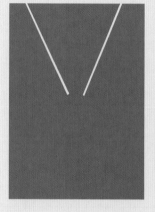

ATTACHING A BLADE
Grip the non-sharp edge of the blade with a pair of tweezers or pliers. Slide the blade onto the handle until it clicks into place. Match up the hole in the blade with the bump on the handle.

REMOVING A BLADE
To safely remove a blade, grip the end of the blade with a pair of tweezers or pliers. Lift the base of the blade away from the handle and carefully slide away.

CUTTING TECHNIQUES

Once you've mastered a few basic principles, craft knives are very easy to use. One of the keys to success is to keep your arms relaxed, so that you can produce fluid movements to get the smoothest cuts.

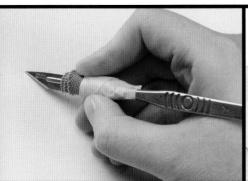

CUT IN COMFORT

Some artists tape masking tape or fabric around the handle of their craft knife, just before the blade, for comfort. This cushions your fingers and prevents the handle from rubbing against your skin.

HOLDING THE CRAFT KNIFE

Hold your craft knife in the same way as a pencil or pen—at about a 45-degree angle to the paper—to give you the best control.

DIRECTION OF CUT

When cutting, always pull the blade toward you; never try to push it away from you.

CUTTING A STRAIGHT EDGE

When cutting a straight edge, always use a metal rule. Your blade will cut into plastic and wooden rulers and leave them uneven and more likely to cause your blade to slip. Place the fingers of your non-cutting hand on the rule, well away from the edge, so that the rule does not slip out of position.

CUTTING A CURVE OR CIRCLE

To cut curves and circles, gently guide the paper around so that the blade is always cutting toward you.

Getting started

Papercuts were traditionally created using scissors and scissors are still used today by many papercutting artists. Here are some of the key skills and techniques that you need to know before getting started.

With the exception of cutting multiples (page 23) and intercutting (page 29), all the projects in this book can be done using either a craft knife or scissors; it is entirely up to you which you use. If you do use scissors, however, there are a couple of things to remember that will make your papercutting life a lot easier.

Scissors come in different shapes and sizes and you will have to try out a few before you can decide which work best for you. You can start by practicing with craft scissors, but to achieve the more detailed and complicated designs, it is advisable to purchase some small, sharp scissors. Embroidery, decoupage, and surgical scissors all work well.

The easiest way to successfully cut with scissors is to sit down, rest your elbows on a table, and hold the piece of paper at eye height in the air. Hold your scissors in one hand; with the other hand, guide the paper into the blades. Keep the hand that is holding the scissors steady and try not to let the blades of the scissors close fully while cutting. This will give you a better line and a smoother finish, avoiding a jagged and rough edge.

Tip
When buying scissors, make sure you select a pair with a grip that fits your hand comfortably.

1 To cut the small, delicate sections of a design, pierce a hole in the area that you are going to remove with the tip of your scissors (they must be sharp). Then make a small snip. Once you have an initial opening, ease your scissors in and carry on cutting.

2 When you have cut the inside sections of the shape, you can begin to cut around the main shape. It is important to cut the inside sections first: once the shape is cut, you will find it difficult to successfully pierce the small, inside areas.

BASIC SCISSOR-CUTTING TECHNIQUES
Small, detailed sections are usually the most difficult parts of a design to cut. Do them first, since your paper will stay whole for longer, which means that it will be stronger and less likely to tear.

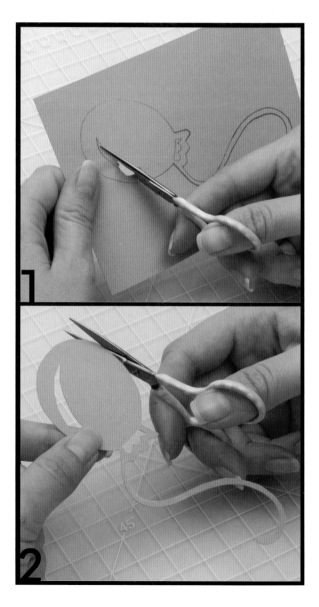

Lots of the projects in this book involve you cutting multiple papercuts. Therefore, it is a good idea to try and cut more than one layer of paper at once to save you some time. Below are a couple of techniques that will help with this. It is best to use a craft knife when cutting through multiple layers as it is difficult to cut internal details through more than one layer using scissors.

ACCORDION FOLDING TECHNIQUE

Accordion folding, or concertina folding, is a great technique to create a line of connected, symmetrical designs. You may have used this technique as a child to create simple garland decorations or paper dolls holding hands. By cutting through layers of folded paper you create a symmetrical design that is great for projects such as the cake wrappers on pages 86–87. It is a good idea to use very thin paper for this technique as you will be cutting through lots of layers at once.

1 Cut a long, thin strip of paper. Fold your paper to create an accordion or concertina. Starting at one end, fold the end of the paper in on itself.

2 Turn the paper strip over and fold the folded end in on itself again, the same distance as the first fold. Repeat this folding until you have folded all your paper.

3 Attach your template, or draw your design directly on to one end of the folded paper. Remember that your design will have to connect all the folds of paper so be careful not to cut completely through the folded edges. In this design the hands are the connecting element. Cut your design out through all the layers of paper using either a craft knife or scissors.

4 Once the design has been cut out, carefully unfold your paper to reveal your chain of symmetrical shapes. Remember that the longer the strip of paper, and the more times you fold it, the more layers you will have to cut through at once.

STACKING TECHNIQUE

This is a simple technique where you stack layers of paper on top of one another and secure them in place, then cut through all the layers to create multiple identical shapes. Consider the weight of the paper when you are choosing how many layers to cut at once so the stack doesn't become too thick to easily cut through. This technique can be used for any project where you need lots of the same shape, such as the party garlands on pages 46–47, the paper wreaths on pages 52–53, and the tree table decorations on pages 54–55.

1 Cut a variety of papers the same size and stack them on top of one another.

2 Secure the papers in place with some invisible tape along at least two edges.

3 Either attach your template onto the top

layer or draw your design directly onto the top layer of paper.

4 Using a craft knife on a cutting mat, cut out your design through all the layers of paper. Cut internal details first as once you cut around the outside, there will be

nothing keeping your layers together. Once the designs have been cut out you will be left with multiple identical shapes, which can be cut from a variety of colors and papers, ready for your project.

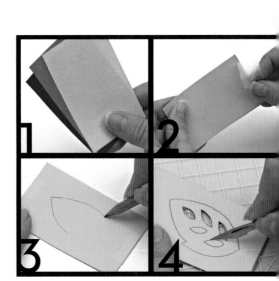

If you are new to papercutting, it is a good idea to use templates, because the design has already been done for you. Once you have grasped the cutting techniques, you can start making your own designs.

This book has been designed so that you can cut the templates straight out of the pages at the back, attach them to your chosen paper, and go. Simply follow the projects step by step and you will end up with some great designs. Alternatively, you can transfer the templates out of the book using one of the methods described on this page.

The solid parts of the templates should be left whole, while the white parts are the areas that you should cut out to reveal your design. Once you have created your final piece, you can keep your template and draw around it again and again to create more designs on different-colored papers.

TRANSFERRING TEMPLATES

If you don't want to cut up this book or you want to re-size the templates there are other ways of transferring a template onto a new piece of paper using carbon paper, tracing vellum, a scanner, or photocopier.

PHOTOCOPYING AND SCANNING

Using a photocopier or scanner is the most common way of transferring a template; it also allows you to play around with the scale of the design. To do this either photocopy your chosen template, or scan it onto your computer, re-size it if desired (see below), and print it out.

Place your chosen paper on a flat surface and attach your printed out template on top, securing the two pieces of paper together with invisible tape to prevent them from slipping out of position while you are cutting. Then all you have to do is cut out your design.

ENLARGING TEMPLATES

Always think about the project you are creating and what size you would like the final papercut to be, as this will influence whether or not you need to scale the template. For some projects, for example the hanging paper rosettes on pages 48–49, you may want to create multiple papercuts at various sizes.

You will notice that a couple of the projects in this book include suggestions for how much you could re-size a template in order to create a finished piece at a particular size.

USING CARBON/GRAPHITE PAPER

You can also trace the template onto your chosen paper using carbon/graphite paper. This means that when you come to do your cutting you only have to cut through one piece of paper—which can make a big difference if you're using thick cardstock. Carbon/graphite paper can be used more than once, so keep it safe after use.

1 Place your chosen paper on a flat surface, with the carbon/graphite paper ink side down on top. Place the photocopied or scanned template on top of the carbon paper. (If you do not have access to a photocopier or scanner, trace the image from the book onto tracing vellum, then use the traced artwork as the top layer.) Secure the three layers together with a sliver of invisible tape so that they cannot slip out of position.

2 Using a sharp implement such as a pencil or pen, draw along the lines of the copied artwork. Once you have drawn all the way around the design, take the layers apart; the image will have been transferred to your chosen paper.

MODIFYING YOUR DESIGN

While you are tracing your design onto your paper, you can modify it a bit and make it your own. Layer your paper, carbon/graphite paper, and template as described above and secure them in place. Trace over the areas of your template that you want to keep and add any new elements you like—as long as anything you add is connected to something else, it will be fine. Remember that any marks you make on your template now will transfer onto your paper via the carbon/graphite paper. If you would like to plan your design first, draw it onto the template before you attach it to the carbon paper, then trace over your new design.

Do you remember making cut-out snowflakes as a child? Well, this is the same principle—a method of cutting that allows you to create a perfectly symmetrical design.

There are lots of different ways to fold paper to create a wide variety of shapes. In papercutting you will mainly come across simple folds that still allow you to cut into the paper easily. There are a few things to consider when cutting a folded design:

The first thing to think about when starting a folded design is what type of paper you are going to use: it should be a lightweight paper that creases well. Origami, the Japanese art of folded paper, often uses a very lightweight paper that is patterned on one side and holds a crease well; this is called "washi" paper.

Whether you are making a single- or a multi-fold design, once you have folded your paper, do not open it out again until you have finished cutting. This not only keeps the element of surprise in your design, but it also means that the paper won't slip out of position—so you'll end up with a more accurate papercut.

Always be aware of where the folded edge of the pattern is: you must make sure that you don't cut all the way along this edge, otherwise your design will fall apart (see right).

SINGLE-FOLD DESIGNS

Fold your chosen paper in half, making sure that the crease is smooth and exact. You should be able to fold it by hand, but if your paper is slightly thicker you can use a bone folder (see page 16).

KEEP THE FOLDED EDGE INTACT

The broken line in this illustration is the folded edge: it's essential that some parts of the design remain in contact with this line, otherwise your papercut will fall apart into two halves.

1 Once your paper is folded in half, start by cutting away the white areas along the dotted line (these are the most important areas as they hold the fold together) and the large white sections of the design.

2 Next, cut away the small, tricky sections within the design.

3 Finally, cut around the outline of the design.

4 Once you have finished cutting your design out, unfold it. It is now that you can see exactly what your final design looks like. When you have completed your design, you may wish to flatten it with an iron set to a low heat.

MULTI-FOLD DESIGNS

Once you have mastered single-fold designs, you can move on to multi-fold designs; these are a lovely way of creating intricate patterns fairly quickly. Multi-fold designs are slightly more difficult because you have to cut through more layers of paper at once, so it is advisable to choose a lighter-weight paper.

TYPES OF PAPER FOLD

Here are some examples of different ways you can fold paper, creating two, four, or eight identical sections. (Remember that the more you fold your paper, the thicker it becomes.)

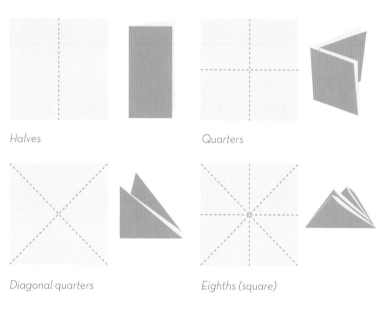

Halves

Quarters

Diagonal quarters

Eighths (square)

Accordion fold

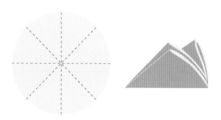

Eighths (circle)

Be very careful when opening out papercuts (especially multi-folds) because the paper can often catch on itself and tear.

MORE THAN ONE FOLD

With multi-fold designs, there is more than just one folded edge to think about. Here, there are two folded edges (indicated by the broken lines). The circles show where the design remains in contact with the folded edges; if all these sections were cut through, the design would fall apart when opened out.

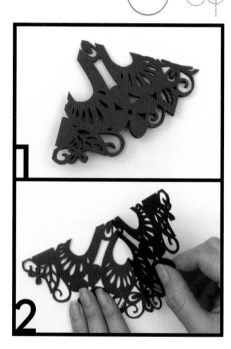

1 Here, the paper has been folded twice, first horizontally and then vertically, into four quarters.

2 As the paper is opened out after cutting, the complexity and symmetry of the design emerges.

SCORING AND INDENTING

Sometimes, you may want to use a heavier paper, which is too thick to fold by hand and can often leave an uneven crease. When this occurs, you can choose to either score or indent your paper to create a smoother crease. Both of the methods shown below are especially useful in cardmaking, so choose whichever method you prefer.

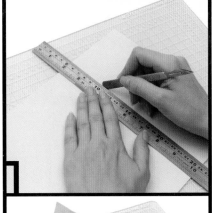

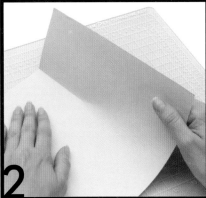

SCORING

This is a technique used to crease heavy paper and thin to medium cardstock. Scoring lightly cuts through the surface of your paper or cardstock, making it easier to fold.

1 Place a metal rule along the center line where you want the fold to be, on what will be the outside surface of the paper. Then very gently slide a craft knife along the edge of the rule, remembering that you only want to cut into the paper on its surface, not all the way through.

2 Turn the paper over and gently fold it in half, with the scored edge on the outside.

3 Press the scored edge with your fingertips or a bone folder to achieve a good, sharp crease.

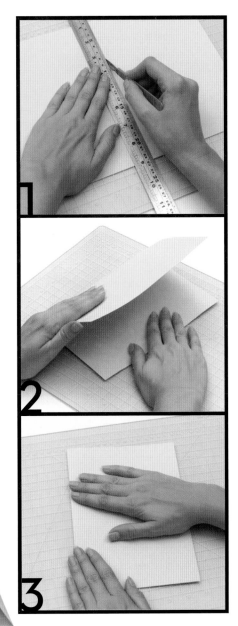

INDENTING

Indenting is used to crease heavy paper and thin to medium cardstock. It is more commonly used in the commercial industry than scoring, and uses pressure to indent a line in the card, making it easier to fold.

1 Place a metal rule along the center line where you would like the crease to be. Instead of cutting into your paper, turn your craft knife upside down and press the handle into the paper along the rule's edge, making sure that you do not break the surface of the paper.

2 Fold the paper in on itself to form a fold, with the indented crease on the inside.

Layering and intercutting are really good ways of adding different colors and depth to your artwork. Both techniques are surprisingly easy to do—and remarkably effective.

LAYERING

Layering means exactly what you would expect it to mean: building up the artwork in stages by superimposing one layer on top of another. There is no limit to the number of layers you can have: you can simply keep adding until you are happy with the result.

One of the great advantages of designing in this way is that, if you make a mistake on one layer, you can either alter the other layers to cover up the mistake, or you can re-do just that one layer. You don't have to re-do the whole design as you would have to in a single-layered cut-out.

There are a few things to take into consideration, however. The first is to remember that you're working from the back toward the front. So if you're creating a simple landscape, for example, the first layer needs to contain the elements that you want to appear to be farthest away—the shapes of distant mountains, perhaps. Then add elements in the middle distance, such as trees. Finally, put in the foreground details—bearing in mind that each layer needs to have a solid base so that you can attach it easily and precisely on top of the previous layers. And, because of the rules of perspective,

1 FIRST LAYER
Here, the flowers that are intended to appear farthest away are cut out first. Note that these flowers are lighter in tone than the subsequent layers—this adds to the appearance of depth.

2 SECOND LAYER
Then the flowers in the middle layer are cut out; this layer is stuck on top of the first, partially covering some elements of the first layer to enhance the feeling of recession and distance.

3 THIRD LAYER
To give the impression that the flowers on the top layer are closer than the previous layers, a darker tone of paper has been used. Place this layer on top of the other two layers, and you are left with a flower garden that is full of detail and depth.

Using layers to create background colors
This is a great way to create a motif for a card or a gift tag, in which the background color shows through the cut-out. See pages 80–81 and 88–89.

1 Cut out a solid shape the same size as your papercut.

2 Stick the papercut on top.

3 The layered papercut consists of two toning colors that complement each other beautifully: it would make a lovely motif for a card or gift tag.

1 Choose two contrasting-colored papers, making sure that they are roughly the same weight.

2 Tape the edges of the papers securely together, so that they cannot slip out of position while you are cutting.

3 Start cutting out your design, remembering to keep hold of the pieces you are removing.

4 Once you have cut out one piece, swap the pieces over and re-attach each one to the opposite color of background paper, using invisible tape on the back of the design.

5 On the finished papercuts, the pieces fit exactly into the holes, giving the impression of a solid piece of paper that is made up of different colors, a bit like a jigsaw puzzle.

you need to think about the size and tone of the layers, too: distant objects should be both smaller and lighter in tone than those in the foreground.

Another thing to consider is how much space there is in the artwork. It is very easy to include too much detail on your first layer and then find that you have no empty space to add new layers. In a simple forest of trees, for example, each layer is very sparse—but when they come together, they create a balanced woodland full of details and depth.

INTERCUTTING

Intercutting is a technique that involves cutting through two pieces of paper at the same time and then swapping over the cut-out sections. It works best when you use two contrasting-colored papers. Once you have cut out your design, tape the cut-out piece back in place on the reverse of your design. Use a craft knife for this technique, as it is difficult to accurately cut through more than one layer to achieve multiple identical pieces using scissors. As you gain more experience and feel comfortable with the technique, you can start adding third, fourth, and even fifth colors—there are no limits.

INTERCUT DESIGNS
Using the intercutting technique you can easily create matching designs in contrasting colors.

When designing your own papercuts, you will have to come to terms with thinking backward. This is because you always draw on the back of the paper, so as not to mark the front of your artwork—so when you turn the paper over, your final design will be the reverse of what you initially drew. Sometimes it can look quite different, while at other times it looks exactly as you thought it would.

LETTERS AND NUMBERS

Thinking backward is really important when you want to include letters and numbers in your designs, because you have to write them backward on your paper. This takes a bit of getting used to, but the more you practice the easier it gets.

When starting a design with text or numbers, plan what you want to include and write it out on a separate piece of paper. Once you have done this, write it out again—this time backward. Rather than thinking about what you are spelling, look at each individual letter or number and what comes next. When writing backward you will find that it is easier to go from the right of your page to the left.

Once you have written out your text backward, you can check it by placing it next to a mirror. When you look in the mirror, your work should look normal. Use your backward text as your reference and copy it into your design.

Another thing to consider when using text and numbers in your artwork is the enclosed spaces within some letters. If your design is going to be a positive design, then this isn't an issue; when you are creating a negative design, however, you will have to either include the centers of the letters afterward or not at all. You will notice that a lot of artists who use text in their work often leave out the centers of their letters. It can add a lovely papercut quality to your work and is worth trying out.

CHANGE OF DIRECTION
When this design was drawn onto the back of the paper (left), the highest balloon was in the top right corner. When the design is cut out (right) and the paper turned over to the right side, the highest balloon is in the top left corner. Changes of direction such as this can have a dramatic effect on the mood of an artwork.

ALPHABET GUIDE
You can use this alphabet as a reference when writing backward because it can be easy to get the letters mixed up. If you want to use it as a template, photocopy or trace it from the book and then use carbon paper to transfer the letters you need for your design (see page 24). Keep this in mind for creating ages for birthday buttons (see pages 74-75) or initials for gift tags (see pages 80-81).

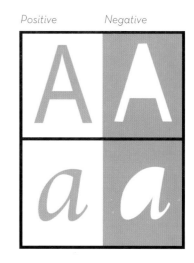

Positive — Negative

CHECK YOUR WORK
Use a mirror to check how your backward letters or numbers will look once they are cut out and flipped.

ENCLOSED SPACES
In the negative design here, the enclosed spaces in the letters will either have to be left out or carefully glued back in place, but they remain in the positive design.

WRITING BACKWARD
As you write, try not to focus on the whole word, but rather think about the shape that each individual letter makes and how this would be reversed.

Tips
- When writing backward, remember to always check your spelling before you start!
- It is important to consider how you space your letters. You do not want the letters to be too close together because this will make them very difficult to cut—but if you space them too wide, the words will not be easily read. There is no firm rule, though, so play around with your lettering: printed, cursive, small, large, capital, or lower case.

Color plays an important part in any craft or art project, and depending on your choice, can totally alter the appearance of your final piece.

It is a good idea to think carefully about the colors you are going to use before you start your projects; by choosing the right colors, you can create the perfect look for any party. For example, if you were hosting a summer garden party you might want to use bright, bold, happy colors such as yellow, orange, and bright pink to add a sense of sunshine. Pastel shades that are lighter, softer, and prettier, such as baby blue and pink,

SPRING

Lighter pastel colors create a soft and innocent feel. These colors are often associated with spring flowers, babies, and all things young and new. By using "spring" colors in your projects, you can create a fresh, spring-time feel that is perfect for bridal and baby showers, Easter celebrations, garden parties, and weddings.

SUMMER

As the weather warms up, brighter, bolder colors such as yellow (the summer sun), bright blue (like summer skies and clear blue seas), and vibrant pinks and purples (for a touch of fiesta) make up the "summer" palette. These colors are often associated with happy, playful, fun times and they will be felt at your summer parties and celebrations.

white, cream, and pale yellow, might be more suited to a baby shower.

A good example of how to alter a project to suit any party just by changing the color is the garland project on pages 46–47. If you were to use black and orange paper, you would immediately have the perfect garland for a Halloween party. Change the colors to red and green and you have a festive garland for Christmas.

There is no right and wrong, but the examples below will give you some ideas as to how different color themes can work well for different occasions. These are organized into seasonal color boards and are only suggestions, but I hope they will help you to choose color themes for your own parties in the future. Each of the projects in this book can be used for more than one type of party simply by changing the color of paper!

FALL

The autumnal colors that are found in nature at this time of year are warm, earthy, and deeper in shade than those of spring and summer. "Fall" colors instantly evoke feelings of crisp mornings, rustling leaves, Halloween trick-or-treating, and cozy Thanksgivings by the fire.

WINTER

Cool colors such as white, icy blue, and silver create a wintry feel and reflect the cold weather of this season. We also associate this time of year with festive times and colors such as red, green, and gold form the basis of a "winter" palette that gives an instant holiday feel to any party.

Motifs are a great way to theme your papercut projects for a specific occasion. With so many celebrations throughout the year, there are plenty of themes to choose from; here are some ideas to get you started.

A lot of the projects in this book can easily be altered to make them suitable for any occasion. Color can play a huge part in changing the look of a project (see page 32)—but so can themed motifs. By using different motifs, you can alter most of the projects in this book to make them suitable for specific parties. For example, the garland project on pages 46-47 can easily be changed to a winter garland by using snowflake motifs rather than the pattered circles, while the hair band project on pages 76-77 could have spiders and cobwebs on it for a Halloween party rather than the flowers shown.

On these pages, I have created four seasonal themes that allow you to change the projects for lots of different parties. I hope these motifs spark your imagination and give you some ideas of what other motifs could be used for the projects in this book. There are no rules and each project can be altered so the list of what can be done is endless—have fun cutting!

SPRING
Included here are motifs that could be used for Easter celebrations, baby showers, and spring parties. Easter eggs, bunny rabbits, daffodils, and tulips are classic spring motifs and can suit numerous occasions.

SUMMER
Garden and beach parties, 4th July celebrations, barbecues, weddings, graduations are all great summer celebrations that these motifs can help represent.

FALL

Halloween and Thanksgiving are key events in the fall and motifs such as black cats, witches, and turkeys are perfect for these celebrations.

WINTER

Festive motifs such as a snowman, reindeer, holly, snowflakes, misteltoe, and candy canes are iconic and can be used all through winter and for all your Christmas parties.

2 PROJECTS

Let all the kids know about your party with this sweet accordion-fold card. This design can be used as an invite or just as a lovely card to send to a child on their birthday! The accordion fold adds some depth to the card, creating a more three-dimensional look.

Tool kit
- Craft knife and blades
- Cutting mat
- Metal rule
- Invisible tape
- Bone folder

Materials
- Thin cardstock differently colored on each side

Choosing materials
This design should stand up on its own when finished, so use thin cardstock rather than paper. It is also a good idea to buy cardstock that is white on one side, so that you can use the white side as the contrasting color.

Template is on page 97

1 Cut out template 3 on page 97. To use the template more than once or to re-size it, photocopy or trace it, following the instructions on page 24.

2 Using a craft knife and metal rule on a cutting mat, cut a piece of thin cardstock the same size as the template.

3 Using invisible tape, fix the template on top of the cardstock, carefully aligning the edges.

4 With the template attached, fold the card along the dotted lines of the template creating a concertina (or into thirds to create an accordion fold if you are not using a template, see page 26). Use your fingers or a bone folder to firmly press down the folds and create sharp creases.

TAKE SPECIAL CARE
Circled in red are the trickiest areas to cut. These areas will be folded so avoid cutting over the folded line.

Tip
When designing your own accordion card, remember to tier the levels and to leave the back page pretty much intact, so that you have room to write your party details or birthday message there.

5 Open the card out flat. Then, using a craft knife on a cutting mat, cut out the white parts of the template and the cardstock at the same time. Pay particular attention when cutting near the folds, because these areas will be under more stress once the card is finished and are more likely to tear.

6 Remove the template and fold the card back into its accordion folds.

7 Now you are ready to write your message on the card. Write your party details or message on the back page, below the balloons, so that it's not visible from the front.

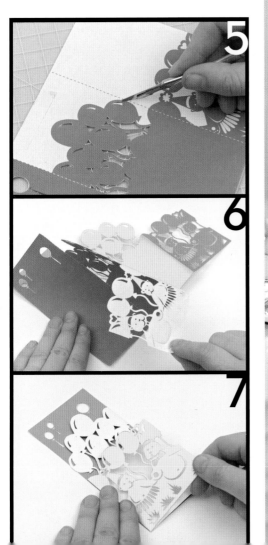

TEDDY BEARS' PICNIC
When displayed, your accordion-fold card will create a fun, layered three-dimensional scene.

GATEFOLD PARTY INVITATION

Invite your friends over for a party using this stylish, floral party invitation—great for weddings, baby showers, bridal showers, or just a lovely summer lunch. On pages 121 and 123, you will find templates for two variations of this design based on the seasons fall and winter, so you have an invitation for parties throughout the year.

Tool kit
- Craft knife and blades
- Cutting mat
- Metal rule
- Bone folder
- Invisible tape
- Spray adhesive
- Glue stick (optional)
- Double-sided tape (optional)

Materials
- Thin cardstock
- Paper in contrasting color for insert
- Thin ribbon (optional)

Choosing materials
This design should stand up on its own when finished, so use a thin cardstock rather than paper; make sure the cardstock is not too thick, because you have to fold it in sections. It is also nice to use a contrasting color for the insert, to add a second color to the design.

Template is on page 121

TAKE SPECIAL CARE
Circled in red are the trickiest areas to cut. The edges of this design will be folded when finished, so be careful not to cut over the folded line.

1   Cut out template 33 on page 121, which is in two parts. To use the templates more than once or to re-size them, photocopy or trace them, following the instructions on page 24.

2   Using a craft knife and metal rule on a cutting mat, cut a piece of thin cardstock the same height as the template and six times the width.

3   Using a bone folder and a metal rule, score (see page 27) and then fold the cardstock into thirds along the dotted lines B and C (see Paper Folds, right). Score and fold each of the two end panels in half again along dotted lines A and D. It is best to do this before you cut out the pattern, so that the card will fold into place more readily at the end.

4   Unfold the card. Using invisible tape and referring to the diagram, attach the templates to the panels on either side of the wide center panel—the first between lines A and B and the second template between lines C and D. Make sure that the two halves of the large center flower are on the outside edges, along lines A and D.

5   Using a craft knife on a cutting mat, cut out the white parts of the template and the card at the same time. Take particular care when cutting along the edges of the design, since these will become the folded edges of the card. Once you have cut out the design, carefully remove the template.

6   Measure the end flap of the card and cut two pieces of a different-colored paper to this size for the inserts.

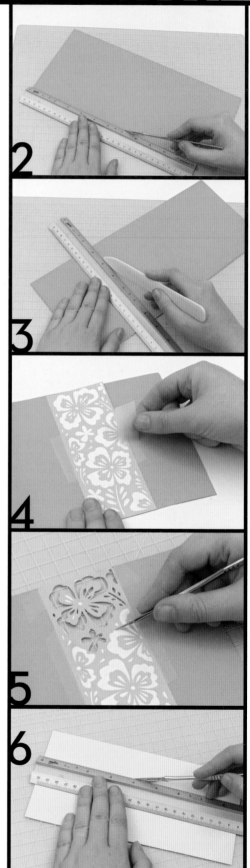

FINISHING TOUCHES
For an extra-special touch, tie some ribbon around the center of the card. This is a lovely feature for a wedding or bridal shower invitation.

7 Using spray adhesive or a glue stick, attach the inserts to the end panels.

8 Spray the backs of the two cut-out panels with adhesive. This is a little tricky, because you don't want to get the spray adhesive anywhere else, so be sure to mask off all other areas of the card with scrap paper beforehand.

9 Fold the insert panels inward, so that they cover the backs of the paper-cut panels. Press down firmly to secure them in place. Next fold the end panels inward again, to meet in the middle. Hand write or print the party details on a separate sheet and attach them to the inside of the card, using double-sided tape or a glue stick.

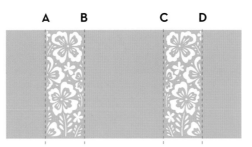

A   B   C   D

PAPER FOLDS
Fold your paper first in thirds at points B and C, then divide the end panels at A and D to help you to accurately place your templates.

POP-UP FESTIVE CARD

Why not add a three-dimensional element to your seasonal greetings cards this year with this pop-up festive design? It will give you the skills you need to create your own pop-up designs in the future.

Tool kit
- Craft knife and blades
- Cutting mat
- Invisible tape
- Metal rule
- Bone folder
- Double-sided tape

Materials
- Two sheets of thin cardstock in contrasting colors

Choosing materials
This design should stand up on its own when finished, so use a thin cardstock rather than paper; make sure the cardstock is not too thick, so that you can easily make the folds that are required to create the pop-up element.

Template is on page 105

1 Cut out template 13 on page 105. To use the template more than once or to re-size it, photocopy or trace it, following the instructions on page 24.

2 Using a craft knife and metal rule on a cutting mat, cut a piece of thin cardstock twice the width of the template.

3 Fold the card in half and use your finger or a bone folder to firmly press down the fold and create a sharp crease. Place the template on the card, aligning the dotted line on the template with the folded edge of the card. Using invisible tape, attach the template to the card.

4 Using a craft knife on a cutting mat, cut out the white parts of the template and the card at the same time. Also cut the solid white lines. Do not cut the dotted lines, as these will be folded.

5 Once all the solid white areas and solid white lines have been cut, fold along the dotted lines. Fold each section of the tree over on itself, using a bone folder to create a sharp crease. Repeat this with all dotted lines.

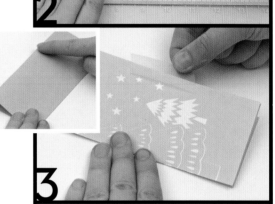

TAKE SPECIAL CARE
Circled in red are the trickiest areas to cut. Remember not to cut the lines that are dotted, as these have to be folded rather than cut to create a successful pop-up.

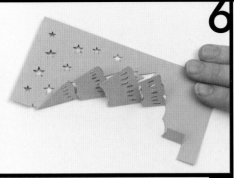

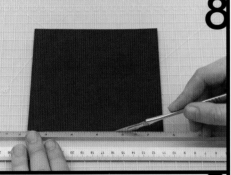

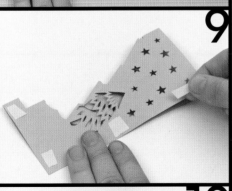

6 Fold back the sections and carefully remove the template.

7 Open out the card and gently pull each section of the tree through to the inside. You will have to re-crease the centerfold line on each section of the tree so that the sections fold the correct way. Repeat this with all sections of the tree and then fold the card in half again to reinforce all the creases.

8 Now you need to make a backing, so that no one sees the pop-up section until they open the card. Cut another piece of thin cardstock in a contrasting color, the same size as the original piece of cardstock. Fold it in half, using your fingers or a bone folder to press down the fold and create a sharp crease.

9 Fold the cut-out card in half along the center crease line, with the pop-up section on the inside. Cut small strips of double-sided tape and place them on the outside of the cut-out card, avoiding the cut out areas.

10 Place the backing paper on the outside of the cut-out card, aligning the center folds. Peel off the backing paper from the double-sided tape and press the backing paper firmly to secure the pop-up section in place.

HAPPY HOLIDAYS
With a personal touch and fun pop-up element, these festive cards are a great way to show people you care this holiday season.

Variation
You may want to decorate the outside of your card rather than leaving it blank. You could attach a paper-cut motif or add text to the outside rather than the inside.

Technically, this isn't a paper-cutting project—but as this decoration can be added to lots of the projects in the book, I felt that it was worth putting it in. It also gives you a chance to explore the pros and cons of working with tissue paper.

Tool kit
- Scissors
- Florist's wire
- Bone folder

Materials
- Tissue paper (about 10 sheets, no more than 25 sheets as it gets a little tricky to pull out the layers)
- String or ribbon to hang the pom-poms up

Choosing materials
Tissue paper is ideal for this project, as it is very thin and can be manipulated into shape by hand. It comes in a wide variety of colors and can be found in most craft and art supply stores.

No template for this project

Tip
If you want to make lots of pom-poms to decorate a room for an event, then it's a good idea to use no more than three colors, or different shades of one color, to keep some unity in the color scheme. Another variation would be to layer different-colored tissue papers to create a multi-colored pom-pom; again, I would stick to three colors as a maximum.

1 Layer about 10 sheets of tissue paper on top of one another. (The number of sheets you use is up to you; the more you use, the more dense your pom-pom will be. I would advise 25 sheets as the maximum.)

2 Fold the tissue-paper stack into accordion folds (see page 26) lengthwise, making each fold about $1^1/_2$ inches (4 cm) deep and making sharp creases along each folded edge as you go. If you have lots of layers of tissue paper, use a bone folder for this.

3 Once all the layers have been folded, fold the stack in half widthwise to create a center crease.

4 Wrap some florist's wire around the center crease line, then twist the wire to secure it in place.

5 Using a pair of scissors, shape the ends of the tissue-paper stack into a curve or a point, depending on your preference.

6 Slowly and carefully start pulling away each layer of tissue from the center. This will take time and you will have to be very careful not to tear the paper. Once all the layers have been teased away from the center, you may need to spend some time tweaking the overall shape to create a more circular pom-pom. Keep gently pulling and fluffing up the paper until you are happy.

7 Once you have finished the pom-pom, decide what length you would like it to hang and cut a length of string or ribbon to size. Loop the string or ribbon under the wire at the center of the pom-pom (you may need to rummage in the ruffles of tissue paper until you find it) and knot it so that you can hang it in its chosen location.

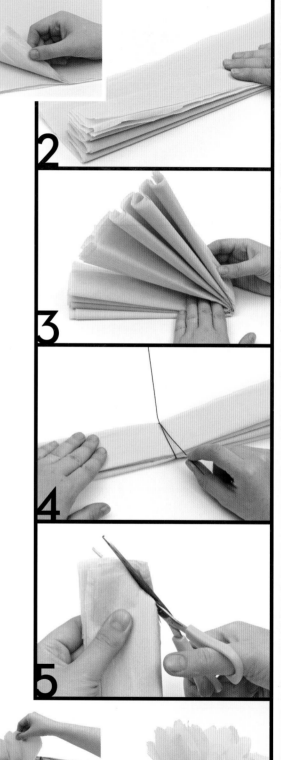

SUMMER DAZE
Use this hassle-free technique to create stunning decorations for your special occasion in any color and any size you like.

PARTY GARLANDS

These simple garlands can be strung up around your home to create beautiful decorations for any party. You may even want to put them up in a child's (or your own) bedroom to add some permanent decorations to a wall or window.

Tool kit
- Craft knife and blades
- Cutting mat
- Invisible tape
- Sewing machine (optional)

Materials
- Paper or thin cardstock
- Needle and thread/ribbon

Choosing materials
You can use any paper or thin cardstock for this project, but if you want to cut out more than one decoration at a time choose a lightweight paper. This means that you can stack the papers together and the pile won't be too thick to cut through.

Template is on page 99

1 Cut out both parts of template 4 on page 99. To use the template more than once or to re-size it, photocopy or trace it, following the instructions on page 24.

2 Using a craft knife and metal rule on a cutting mat, cut a piece of colored paper to fit each part of the template. Using invisible tape, attach the templates to the paper. To cut more than one decoration at a time, stack several pieces of colored paper together and secure the edges with invisible tape to keep them in place (see page 23).

3 Using a craft knife on a cutting mat, cut out the white parts of the template and the paper(s) at the same time, starting with the small inner details. Carefully cut around the outside edge; if you prefer, you can use scissors for this rather than a craft knife. Remove the template.

4 Repeat step 3 until you have enough decorations to make your garland; you may need more than you think.

TAKE SPECIAL CARE
The areas circled in red are the areas to pay closest attention to; you will need to pierce a small hole in these areas with your needle, so they need to be left uncut.

Variations
- Think about using different patterned papers for your garlands. Old music scores and pages from old books would give a lovely vintage feel to your decorations. Alternatively, make some mini pom-poms (see pages 44–45) and add them to your garlands among the papercut shapes.
- Instead of using a needle and thread, you can use a sewing machine to join all the decorations together. Set up your sewing machine with your chosen color of thread and sew through the center of each decoration, leaving the required length of thread between each decoration.

GARLANDS GALORE
Using different color cardstock and varying the shape, size, and number of decorations means this garland can be as subtle or as show-stopping as you want it to be.

5 Thread a needle with your chosen color of thread or very thin ribbon and knot the end at the point where you want the first decoration to go. (Remember to leave space at each end of the thread, so that you can hang the garland.) Pierce the center of the first decoration (or the point marked X on the template, depending on which template you are using) with the needle and slide the decoration all the way to the end of the thread, where you tied the knot. Tie another knot on the other side of the decoration to prevent it from sliding along the thread.

6 Repeat step 5, spacing the decorations evenly, until your garland is the length you want.

Projects

These decorations look lovely hanging from a window or grouped together above a table to create a centerpiece for the room; alternatively, make miniature versions to hang from a festive tree. I have added paper-cut details to mine, but they also look lovely as plain folded paper rosettes.

Tool kit
• Invisible tape
• Scissors
• Double-sided tape
• Needle

Materials
• Three sheets of lightweight paper (all the same size and color) for each rosette
• String or ribbon to hang the rosettes up

Choosing materials
As you have to make lots of folds for this project, use a lightweight paper. Although you are using three sheets of paper, I recommend that they are all the same color or pattern, so that the final rosette looks like one large piece of paper.

Template is on page 105

TAKE SPECIAL CARE
Circled in red are the trickiest areas to cut. Be careful not to overcut the areas on the fold otherwise the design will not hold together when unfolded.

1 Cut out template 11 on page 105. To use the template more than once or to re-size it, photocopy or trace it, following the instructions on page 24.

2 With a bone folder, accordion fold (see page 26) your three sheets of paper lengthwise, one at a time, so that the folds are the same width as the template (about ³/₄ inch/2 cm). Make sure that you make the same number of folds in each piece of paper.

3 Fold each of the paper concertinas in half widthwise, pressing down firmly to make a sharp center crease.

4 Using invisible tape, attach the template to one of the folded sheets of paper, aligning the dotted line on the template with the center fold you have just made.

5 Using a pair of scissors, cut out the white areas of the template and the first folded sheet of paper at the same time. Unless you are using very lightweight paper, it is advisable to use scissors rather than a craft knife for this project as you are cutting through so many folded layers. Remove the template and repeat with the other two folded pieces of paper.

6 Open out the center crease. Attach a piece of double-sided tape along the edge of the folded paper on one side of the center crease, then peel off the backing paper and press the other half of the folded paper strip on top.

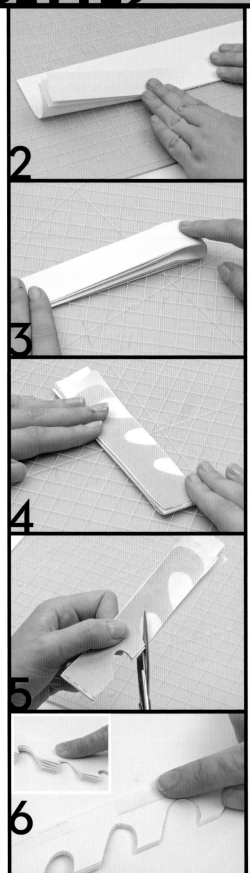

7 Repeat step 6 with each folded
section in turn, then secure all
three sections together in the same way
to create one full circular paper rosette.
(If you want to keep your decorations
flat until the party, then leave the two
final sections unstuck until you are ready
to hang them.)

8 Once you have finished your
rosettes, pierce a small hole in the
top of each one with a needle or a craft
knife and thread through some ribbon so
that you can hang them.

Tip
If you are planning to make lots
of these for a big party, then it's a
good idea to partially complete
them up to step 7, leaving the
final two sides unstuck until you
are ready to hang them. This way
you can store them flat, which
saves room and prevents the
decorations from getting
squashed or damaged.

PERSONAL TOUCH
Hang your finished
rosettes individually or
in clusters of odd numbers
for a really lovely
homemade decoration,
in a variety of colors,
sizes, and motifs.

Using papercuts as hanging window decorations is a very traditional way of displaying them and a great way of creating decorations to adorn your home. The templates in this book represent the four seasons—spring, summer, fall, and winter—so can be used throughout the year. They would also make lovely decorations for a festive tree if created in white.

Tool kit
- Craft knife and blades
- Cutting mat
- Invisible tape
- Needle
- Scissors

Materials
- Colored paper or thin cardstock
- Thread or ribbon

Choosing materials
You can use either paper or thin cardstock for this project, depending on how confident you are with your craft knife. Remember that it is easier to cut through paper than thin cardstock, especially on the intricately detailed sections.

Template is on page 135

TAKE SPECIAL CARE
Circled in black are the trickiest areas to cut. Pay special attention to the areas that connect the squirrel to the border.

1 Cut out template 52 on page 135. To use the template more than once or to re-size it, photocopy or trace it, following the instructions on page 24.

2 Cut a piece of paper to fit the template. Using invisible tape, attach the template to the paper.

3 Using a craft knife on a cutting mat, cut out the white parts of the template and the paper at the same time. The designs are quite detailed, so take your time. Start by cutting the smaller details in the center of the design before cutting the outside edge.

4 Remove the template to reveal the finished design. You could leave it at this stage and frame it or store it flat—but if you want to hang it straight away, follow step 5.

5 Decide how long the hanging thread needs to be and cut it to the required length. Using a needle, pierce a small hole through the paper at the top of your paper-cut design. Thread the needle with thread or thin ribbon, then take the needle through this hole. Create a small loop around the paper-cut design and knot it so that the thread or ribbon stays in place. The decoration is now ready to hang from a window, mantel shelf, or banister to decorate your home.

DOUBLE-SIDED ART
A papercut attached to a window is a double treat as it can be enjoyed from inside and outside the house.

Variation
The designs on pages 133–137 come in two size options, which can be used to different effect. I would recommend enlarging the templates on page 137 by 200% to create a window decoration. Alternatively, you can keep them small and use them as Christmas tree decorations or as motifs on the front of greetings cards. Just remember that the smaller the design is, the harder the cutting will be so take your time and use thin paper to make it easier.

Wreaths are a lovely way to decorate your home, and although they are mostly associated with Christmas, they can be used throughout the year. By using paper leaves rather then real ones, you can use the wreath again and again as the leaves won't wilt.

Tool kit
- Craft knife and blades
- Cutting mat
- Metal rule
- Invisible tape
- Bowls to draw around
- Scissors
- Double-sided tape
- Stapler and staples, plus a bone folder (optional)

Materials
- Colored paper
- Thick cardstock
- Ribbon

Choosing materials
By carefully selecting the colors of the paper you use, you can create a wreath to suit every occasion. A white-and-silver wreath would make a lovely winter decoration; a mixture of yellow, red, and brown, like the example shown here, is perfect for Thanksgiving; or how about orange and black leaves for Halloween? You could even create a romantic wreath, using the heart-shaped templates on page 103, to decorate the interior of your home on Valentine's day.

Template is on page 103

TAKE SPECIAL CARE
Circled in black is the trickiest area to cut. Be careful not to cut off the delicate stems on your leaves.

1 Cut out all the parts of template 9 on page 103. To use the templates more than once or to re-size them, photocopy or trace them, following the instructions on page 24.

2 Choose either one colored paper or a selection of three colors that you think complement each other or match your party theme. You will need enough paper to make 30–50 leaves, so make sure you have enough ready before you start.

3 Using invisible tape, attach the template to the paper. If the paper you are using is not too thick, you can layer two or three sheets and cut out several leaves at the same time. Secure layered sheets of paper together by placing small pieces of invisible tape along the edges (see page 23).

4 Using a craft knife on a cutting mat (or scissors), cut out the leaves, remembering to cut out the small details within the leaves. Carefully remove the template.

5 Repeat step 4 with each of the leaf templates until you have enough leaves to make a wreath. You will need 30–50 leaves, depending on how big you want the wreath to be.

6 Next, make a base for your wreath using a large piece of thick cardstock. Decide how big you want the wreath to be and draw a circle on the cardstock; turning a large mixing bowl upside down and drawing around it will give you a good-sized circle. Then draw another, smaller circle inside the first one (you could draw around another, slightly smaller bowl for this), creating a ring approximately 2–3 inches (5–8 cm) deep.

7 Cut out the ring using a pair of scissors or a craft knife on a cutting mat. Then cut two small holes in the top of the cardstock base, about 3–4 inches (8–10 cm) apart. This is so that you can attach a ribbon later.

8 Place a small piece of double-sided tape on the bottom of each leaf. Choose a point on your base to begin, peel the backing off the double-sided tape on your first leaf, and press the leaf down onto the cardstock base.

9 Slowly build up your leaves, moving around the circle as you go and remembering to cover all the base. The leaves should follow the curve of the base and should closely overlap one another to create a full-looking wreath with no gaps.

10 Take a piece of ribbon in a complementary color, thread it through one of the holes in the base from the front, and then bring it out of the other hole from the back. Tie the ends of the ribbon together in a bow to create a loop. Now the wreath can be hung on your front door to welcome guests into your home.

FALLING LEAVES
The reds, yellows, and browns on this wreath make it a perfect decoration in those crisp fall months.

Tip
To add depth to your wreath, fold each leaf in half lengthwise, using a bone folder, and then open them up before you attach them to the wreath base. This will create a 3-D look. To attach folded leaves, use a stapler rather than double-sided tape to make sure that each leaf is securely fastened to your cardstock backing board.

TREE TABLE DECORATIONS

These tree decorations can be used to decorate any window ledge, mantel shelf, or table top at any time of the year, but would work especially well in the winter. You could create your own mini forest by making lots of them in different sizes for a really lovely festive centerpiece to a party table.

Tool kit
- Craft knife and blades
- Cutting mat
- Invisible tape
- Sewing machine and thread
- Bone folder

Materials
- Colored paper (3 sheets for each tree)

Choosing materials
Medium paper, rather than cardstock, is best for this project, as you have to be able to sew through three layers of it on your sewing machine.

Template is on page 101

TAKE SPECIAL CARE
Circled in red are the trickiest areas to cut. Small details can be fiddly, so take your time when cutting the details on the trees, especially if you are cutting through more than one layer of paper at once.

1 Cut out template 8 on page 101. To use the template more than once or to re-size it, photocopy or trace it, following the instructions on page 24.

2 Using a craft knife and metal rule on a cutting mat, cut a piece of paper in your chosen color to fit the template. Using invisible tape, attach the template to the paper. If your paper is thin enough to allow you to cut more than one at once, layer all three sheets on top of one another and secure at the sides with invisible tape. Then attach the template to the top of the stack (see page 23).

3 Using a craft knife on a cutting mat, cut out the white parts of the template and the paper at the same time. Cut the smaller details in the tree first, then cut around the outside edge. Remove the template.

4 If you didn't layer your papers in step 2, repeat steps 2 and 3 with the other two papers. Layer all three trees on top of one another.

5 Thread your sewing machine with a thread that matches the paper color. Sew down the center of the three layers of trees from the bottom to the top.

6

7

6 Carefully fold the tree on the top of the stack over along the center stitching line and run a bone folder over the fold to create a crease. Turn the trees over and repeat with the tree that was on the bottom of the stack.

7 Tweak the sides of the tree so that the sides are evenly spaced and the tree can stand on its own. Repeat the project until you have a small woodland decorating the center of your table.

Variation
You can still make these tree decorations even if you don't have a sewing machine. Instead of making three cut-out trees, just make two. On the first tree, cut a slit from the top down to the center; on the second, cut a slit from the bottom up to the center. Then slot one tree onto the other at a 90-degree angle, so that they are locked together (see below).

OH CHRISTMAS TREE
Co-ordinate your tree decorations with your party theme. Mix subtle, icy tones with bright reds and lucious golds for a festive treat that everyone will love.

Why not add some smiles to your guest's faces by having them pose for some photos with these dress-up props. The glasses and moustaches will add a fun element to your party—and children will love them, too. Think of the cute photos you can get of your friends and family with these little added extras.

Tool kit
- Craft knife and blades
- Cutting mat
- Invisible tape

Materials
- Medium cardstock
- Wooden sticks

Choosing materials
A medium cardstock works best for this project, as the props need to be fairly rigid so that they won't flop around and fall flat. The templates have been designed so that there aren't too many small details, so you can easily cut them out of card rather than paper. Add feathers, glitter, or sequins to the glasses for an extra-special detail.

Template is on page 141

1 Cut out template 57 on page 141. To use the template more than once or to re-size it, photocopy or trace it, following the instructions on page 24.

2 Using a craft knife and metal rule on a cutting mat, cut a piece of cardstock to fit the template. Using invisible tape, attach the template to the cardstock.

3 Using a craft knife on a cutting mat, cut out the white parts of the template and the cardstock at the same time. Cut out the center of the eyeglasses and the small white details first, before cutting around the outside edge.

4 Carefully remove the template to reveal the cut-out glasses.

5 Turn the glasses over. Using a small piece of invisible tape, attach a wooden stick to either the left- or the right-hand side. Now your prop is ready for its first photo shoot!

TAKE SPECIAL CARE
Be careful when cutting around the bridge of the glasses that keeps the two sides together. Don't cut this part too thin or the glasses may bend and hang limply.

Variation
You could create a whole array of different props to add to your dress-up box and bring them out at lots of different occasions to bring a smile to someone's face. Why not make animal-themed props to turn the noses of your family and friends into the snouts of a variety of furry animals for the party?

WACKY FACES
People won't be able to resist playing with your wacky party props and pulling some silly faces for the camera.

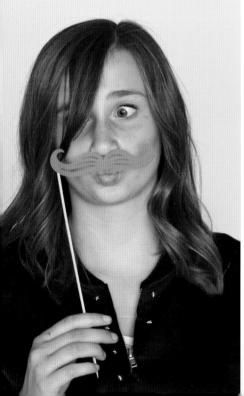

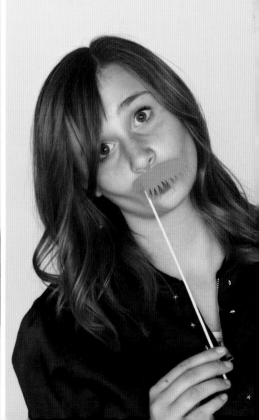

This is a great project to add some fun decorations to your party table. You could also use the pinwheels as cake toppers by skewering them to the tops of a cake or cupcakes before arranging them on a cake stand.

Tool kit
- Craft knife and blades
- Cutting mat
- Invisible tape
- Metal rule
- Pencil

Materials
- Paper that is a different color on each side
- Brass paper fasteners (available from stationery stores)
- Wooden sticks or toothpicks (depending on size of pinwheels)

Choosing materials
Use a paper that is a different color on each side, so that you get a contrasting color within the folds of your pinwheel. Paper that is colored on one side and white on the other is also an easy way to achieve this effect.

Template is on page 123

1 Cut out template 36 on page 123. To use the template more than once or to re-size it, photocopy or trace it, following the instructions on page 24.

2 Using a craft knife and metal rule on a cutting mat, cut a piece of paper the same size as the template. Using invisible tape, fix the template on top of the paper, carefully aligning the edges.

3 Using a craft knife on a cutting mat, cut out the small white parts of the template and the paper at the same time. Next, cut the diagonal solid lines (inset), being careful to cut only the length of the line, not all the way into the center. (If you are designing your own pinwheel rather than using a template, draw two diagonal lines from corner to corner to create an "X." This "X" will be your cut guide and you must remember not to cut fully into the center.)

4 Using a craft knife, cut small crosses where marked on the template—one in each corner and one in the center—to allow the brass paper fasteners through easily. Cut around the outside edge of the template.

TAKE SPECIAL CARE
Circled in red are the trickiest areas to cut. It's very important that you only cut the length of the lines, not all the way into the center, or your pinwheel will wind up in four pieces.

5 Remove the template. One by one bring each of the four corners into the center, aligning the crosses on top of one another. Once aligned, carefully push a brass fastener through all of the layers to keep the corners in place.

6 Turn the pinwheel over and bend back the arms of the fastener so that the blades of your pinwheel are secured in place.

7 Attach a thin wooden stick (or a toothpick if you are making very small pinwheels) on to the back of each pinwheel using invisible tape. Now they are ready to be placed in glasses or vases as decorations, given to children to play with, or pushed down into the tops of cakes to create some fun cake toppers.

Variation
Make different sizes of pinwheels to add to other decorations. Mini pinwheels attached to toothpicks would be great as cupcake toppers or look sweet as buttonholes for men's jackets.

COLORFUL CREATIONS
As these decorations are fun and representative of childhood toys; think about using bright, bold colors such as red, pink, and yellow to reflect this feeling.

WINTER WONDERLAND
*The festive season is a great
time for staying out of the
cold, snuggling by the fire,
and letting your creative
side flourish by making some
papercut decorations.*

Projects

This is a very simple little project that adds a little extra touch to your party table. Not only do the food flags look nice, but they also let your guests know what food is on offer, so they can choose which yummy delights to enjoy!

Tool kit
• Craft knife and blades
• Cutting mat
• Invisible tape
• Double-sided tape
• Bone folder

Materials
• Thin cardstock or paper
• Toothpick

Choosing materials
If you want to be able to use your food flags more than once, use a thin cardstock rather than paper, so that they will be stronger.

Template is on page 119

1 Cut out template 31 on page 119. To use the template more than once or to re-size it, photocopy or trace it, following the instructions on page 24.

2 Using a craft knife and metal rule on a cutting mat, cut a piece of cardstock or paper slightly larger all round than the template. Using invisible tape, attach the template to the cardstock or paper.

3 Using a craft knife on a cutting mat, cut out the white inner details in the template and the cardstock at the same time. If you are feeling brave, cut through two layers of cardstock at once to make more than one flag at a time and save time (see page 23).

4 Carefully cut around the outside edges. Remove the template.

5 Carefully fold the flag in half, matching the outside edges together, and press with your fingers. Open the flag out. Using a bone folder, make a sharp crease down the center.

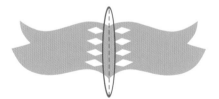

TAKE SPECIAL CARE
Circled in red are the trickiest areas to cut. This area will be folded so avoid cutting over the folded line.

Variation
If you are not going to write the recipe title on your flag, then try using a patterned paper or cardstock for this project. Then the flags can be used as pretty cupcake toppers instead.

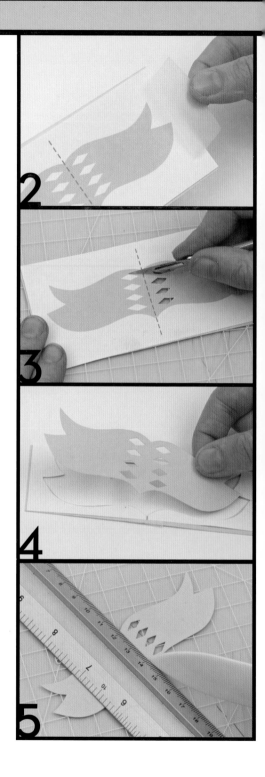

6 Unfold the flag again, place a toothpick in the folded crease line, and stick it in place with a small piece of invisible tape.

7 Place a piece of double-sided tape or other form of adhesive on one side of the inside of your flag, fold the other side of the flag over it, and press down to secure it in place. Now your food flag is ready for you to write the recipe title on the outside—or to place it in the top of a cupcake as an extra decoration.

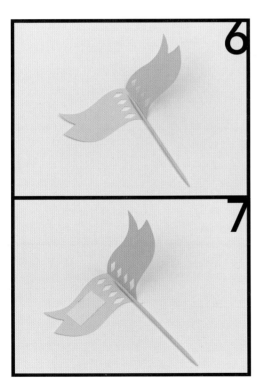

FLYING THE FLAG

How you use your finished flags is up to you. You could add warnings for vegetarians or allergy sufferers, give each recipe a restaurant menu-style name, or make your guests guess the ingredients by drawing your own pictures on the flags.

These napkin holders are a lovely way to add detail to your festive table, and work really well for weddings, too. By changing the colors or motif, the napkin holders can be used for a wide range of special occasions.

Tool kit
- Craft knife and blade
- Cutting mat
- Metal rule
- Invisible tape

Materials
- Thin cardstock

Choosing materials
Thin cardstock rather than paper is advised for this project to give your napkin holders extra strength; this means that you should be able to use them again and again.

Template is on page 107

TAKE SPECIAL CARE
Be careful when cutting the slits at each end of the template, as these form the tab that joins the sides of the napkin holder together and keeps it in place.

1 Cut out template 14 on page 107. To use the template more than once or to re-size it, photocopy or trace it, following the instructions on page 24.

2 Cut a piece of cardstock to fit the template. Using invisible tape, attach the template to the cardstock.

3 Using a craft knife on a cutting mat, cut out the white inner details in the template and the cardstock at the same time. If you are feeling brave, try cutting through two layers of cardstock at once to save time (see page 23).

4 Carefully cut the slits at each end of the template. Use a metal rule to help you keep your cut straight.

5 Cut around the outside edges, then remove the template.

6 Slot the two ends into each other at a 90-degree angle, so that the ends are locked together. Now all you have to do is roll your napkin into a tube shape and carefully put it into the napkin holder.

Variation
These napkin holders can also double up as place setting cards. To do this, don't cut out the details in the butterfly wings; instead, leave them blank so that you have space to write your guests' names.

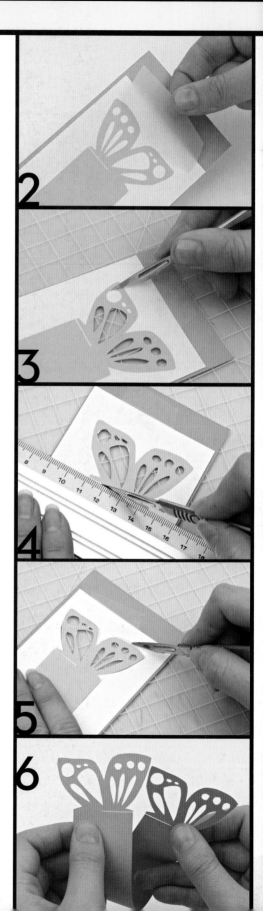

PICK FOR YOUR PARTY
This butterfly design is perfect for a birthday or a summer's lunch, but check out the other templates on page 107 and find a design that suits your occasion.

This corsage can be added to any outfit to make it all the more special and, because it is made from paper rather then the real thing, it will last—so you can use it again and again.

Tool kit
- Craft knife and blades
- Cutting mat
- Invisible tape
- Double-sided tape
- Low-tack poster putty (optional)
- Needle and thread (optional)

Materials
- Thin cardstock or paper in different colors
- Brooch pin

Choosing materials
Try playing around with different weights of paper for this project, as each type will give you a different effect. My only recommendation is to make the bottom layer (usually the leaves) from thin cardstock rather than paper, so that the brooch pin has something strong to attach to.

Template is on page 111

TAKE SPECIAL CARE
Circled in red and black are the trickiest areas to cut. Some of the designs in this papercut are very small and intricate so be careful and take your time.

1 Cut out all the parts of template 22 on page 111. To use the templates more than once or to re-size them, photocopy or trace them, following the instructions on page 24.

2 Attach the templates to your chosen paper by securing around the edges with invisible tape. Think about what colors you are using for each template: make the petals one color, the center circle of the flower a second color, and the leaves a third color.

3 Using a craft knife on a cutting mat, cut out the white inner details in the templates and the paper at the same time.

4 Carefully cut around the outside edges, then remove the template. Repeat steps 3 and 4 until you have cut out all the different flower components.

5 Now start assembling the corsage. Place a piece of double sided tape on the bottom of each petal, then peel off the backing paper and attach it to the center of the three-petal base. Repeat until all the petals have been attached. You may want to bend each petal upward slightly before you stick it in place, to make the corsage more three-dimensional.

6 Now attach the leaves to the back of the flower in the same way.

7 Finally, attach the flower center.

8 Turn your corsage over and tape a brooch pin to the back of the flower, making sure that you can open and close the pin. Now all you have to do is choose an outfit to match the corsage! Instead of attaching the flower to a brooch pin, why not attach it to a length of ribbon so it can be tied around your wrist, a bag, or worn in your hair.

Tip
If you want to secure your pieces together more firmly, you may want to sew them in place. Place the corsage on a small piece of low-tack poster putty. Using a needle, pierce four small holes in a cross shape through all layers of paper. Thread the needle, knot the end of the thread, and stitch through the holes to secure the layers of paper together. I find that a small cross stitch works well and looks good.

FUNKY FLOWERS
This is a great project to experiment with color. Don't be bound by realism—try patterned paper, or multi-colored leaves for a modern, fun twist.

CAKE TOPPERS

Adorn the tops of your cakes with these special paper decorations: they make the perfect embellishments for wedding cakes, birthday cakes, and cakes for any other special occasion you can think of. You can also choose template 18 on page 109 and make smaller toppers to go on top of cupcakes.

Tool kit
- Craft knife and blades
- Cutting mat
- Invisible tape

Materials
- Thin cardstock
- Toothpicks
- Cake or cupcakes

Choosing materials
To ensure that your cake toppers will stay upright, use cardstock rather than paper. This also means they will be stronger so you could use them again and again. Alternatively you could treasure them as a keepsake as a little reminder of the special day.

Template is on page 109

1 Cut out template 17 on page 109. To use the template more than once or to re-size it, photocopy or trace it, following the instructions on page 24.

2 Cut a piece of cardstock to fit the template. Using invisible tape, attach the template to the cardstock.

3 Using a craft knife on a cutting mat, cut out all the white details on the template and the card at the same time.

4 Carefully cut around the outside edge of the topper, then remove the template.

5 Turn the topper over. Depending on the size of the topper, place either one or two toothpicks on the back and secure in place with a small piece of invisible tape.

6 If you are using the ribbon-style toppers, write a personal message on them—Happy Birthday, the name of the birthday boy or girl, the names of the wedding couple, or maybe the date of the wedding or special occasion. Now all you need to do is bake or buy some cakes and attach these toppers to them to add a personal homemade touch.

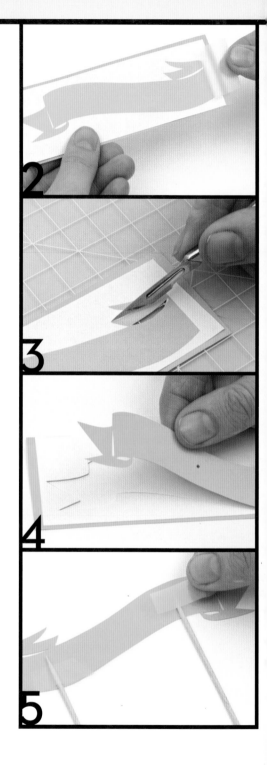

Variation
Rather than creating a banner-style topper with space for a message, you could create a motif topper using the bird or heart templates on page 109, which would make lovely wedding cake toppers, for example. Alternatively, have a look at the suggested motifs on pages 34–35 and come up with something of your own that would suit your special occasion.

TAKE SPECIAL CARE
Circled in red are the trickiest areas to cut. These only need to be very thin slits. Be careful not to overcut and risk cutting a whole corner off your banner.

TASTY TREATS
Whatever the occasion, use this cake topper banner to add a personal message to the top of your cake.

PLACE CARDS

These pretty little place cards can be used on their own or in conjunction with the co-ordinating placemats on pages 72–73.

Tool kit
- Craft knife and blades
- Cutting mat
- Metal rule
- Invisible tape
- Bone folder (optional)

Materials
- Thin cardstock
- Ribbon (optional)

Choosing materials
Use cardstock rather than paper for this project, so that the cards will stand up. When choosing the color of the cardstock, remember that it needs to be light enough for you to be able to write on. If you do want to use a dark color cardstock, try writing your guests' names in a silver pen.

Template is on page 111

1 Cut out template 25 on page 111. To use the template more than once or to re-size it, photocopy or trace it, following the instructions on page 24.

2 Using a craft knife and a metal rule on a cutting mat, cut out a rectangle of cardstock the same size as the template.

3 Using invisible tape, attach the template to the cardstock.

4 Using a craft knife on a cutting mat, carefully cut out the white snowflake details on the template and the cardstock at the same time. Next, cut out the outline around the snowflake, remembering that you only need to cut one side; this is shown as a white line on the template.

5 Remove the template. Place a metal rule along the center of the design (where the dotted line is on the template). Using a craft knife or a bone folder, gently score the folding edge on either side of the snowflake, being careful not to cut through the cardstock or through the snowflake design.

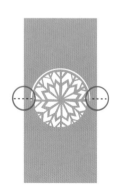

TAKE SPECIAL CARE
Score and fold along the dotted line, but remember you must not fold the snowflake design.

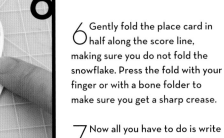

6 Gently fold the place card in half along the score line, making sure you do not fold the snowflake. Press the fold with your finger or with a bone folder to make sure you get a sharp crease.

7 Now all you have to do is write your guests' names on the front of the cards and place them on the table.

TAKE YOUR SEATS
Pick the color and motif that most closely suits your occasion and add an elegant and personal touch to the table at any dinner party.

Variation
I have included some alternative designs in the template section (page 111), so you can choose a motif to match the theme of your party. If you wish, you can attach a small piece of ribbon to the front of the place cards to make them extra special; if you do, you will have to write your guests' names inside the place cards rather than on the outside.

72 PLACEMATS

These simple placemats look great for a special dinner party—especially if you co-ordinate them with the napkin holders and place cards on pages 64–65 and 70–71. To make sure you get plenty of use out of them, it might be worth laminating them so that any little marks can be wiped away at the end of the meal.

Tool kit
- Craft knife and blades
- Cutting mat
- Metal rule
- Invisible tape

Materials
- Thin cardstock or paper

Choosing materials
You can use any paper for this project—but if you want to cut out more than one at a time, use a lightweight paper so that, when you stack the papers, they won't be too thick for you to cut through all the layers. If you choose to laminate the placemats, this will add extra weight and strength, so a lightweight paper is fine.

Template is on page 115

1 Cut out template 27 on page 115. As there is detail only in one corner of this design, the full placemat is not shown and you can determine the finished size in step 2. To use the template more than once or to re-size it, photocopy or trace it, following the instructions on page 24.

2 Cut a piece of paper that is slightly larger than the final size you would like your placemat to be. As a guide, 12 inches x 10 inches (30 cm x 25 cm) would work well. Attach your template to the top left-hand corner of your paper using invisible tape, making sure that the detail is on the paper, not hanging over the edge. To cut more than one placemat at a time, stack the paper and secure the edges with invisible tape (see page 23).

3 Using a craft knife on a cutting mat, cut out all the white details on the template and the paper at the same time.

4 Cut along lines A and B on the template using a craft knife on a cutting mat, and extend the lines to the edges of your paper. Make sure these edges are nice and straight by using a metal rule.

5 Remove the template. Repeat steps 2–4 until you have enough placemats for your table. You could then consider laminating them so they can be used again and again.

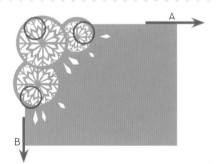

A
B

TAKE SPECIAL CARE
The snowflake design is very intricate with a lot of thin, delicate lines. Be careful not to cut these lines too far, so that all the areas are connected to each other securely and the whole design holds together.

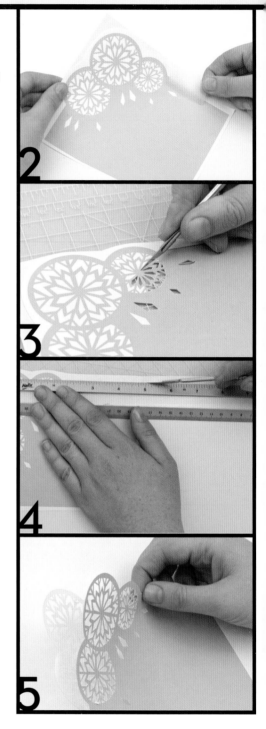

SETTINGS WITH STYLE
Whether you laminate your placemats and use them again and again, or create a personalized design for that extra special occasion, these add a lovely touch to your table.

BIRTHDAY BUTTONS

Why not let everyone know who the birthday boy or girl is by making one of these papercut birthday buttons? You can add their name or their age to the front; either way, everyone will know it's their special day.

Tool kit
- Craft knife and blades
- Cutting mat
- Invisible tape
- Scissors

Materials
- Thin cardstock in different colors
- Double-sided tape, foam sticky dots, or other adhesive
- Button pin

Choosing materials
These are designed for a child's birthday so think about the colors you choose—bright, bold colors are eye-catching and fun. Have a look at the color suggestions on pages 32–33 to give you some ideas. Also, think about using cardstock rather than paper so that the buttons are strong and will withstand a lot of wear and tear.

Template is on page 125

TAKE SPECIAL CARE
Take care with the placement of the layers of your button. You want to see each of the stars' points individually, and evenly spaced around the button.

1 Cut out all the parts of template 42 on page 125. To use the templates more than once or to re-size them, photocopy or trace them, following the instructions on page 24.

2 Using a craft knife and metal rule on a cutting mat, cut a piece of cardstock to fit the template. Using invisible tape, attach the star template to the cardstock. Then, using a craft knife on a cutting mat, carefully cut out the white inner details of the template and the cardstock at the same time.

3 Cut around the outside edge of the template and cardstock, then remove the template.

4 Repeat steps 2 and 3, first using the star template with diamond-shaped cuts and a different color of cardstock, and then with the jagged circle template and a third color of cardstock, so that you have the three components of the button.

5 Now stick the layers together using double-sided tape or, as I have done, sticky foam dots to give your button a more three-dimensional look. Make sure that the points of the second star sit evenly between the points of the first star.

6

7

Variation
Why not make buttons
to use as name cards
at a wedding—they
make really great
conversation starters.

6 Turn the button over so that
the back is facing upward and
place the button pin in the center.
Place a small piece of invisible
tape across the bar of the pin,
making sure it can still open and
close easily.

7 Now the button is ready for
you to write the name of the
birthday person on the front.
Alternatively, cut out their age
from cardstock and attach it to the
front of the button with a sticky
foam dot. You can use the guide on
page 31 to draw or photocopy a
template for an age or initial.

IT'S MY PARTY
*Choose the birthday girl or
boy's favorite colors for an
even bigger smile on that
special day.*

PARTY HAIR BAND

Compared to the traditional party hat, these hair bands will add a touch of fun and glamour to any party. They can be made for adults and children alike and, by changing the colors of the paper, or the motifs, can be used as an accessory for lots of different parties!

Tool kit
- Craft knife and blade
- Cutting mat
- Invisible tape
- Scissors
- Double-sided tape or other adhesive

Materials
- Paper in a variety of colors and weights
- Old hair band
- Craft wire (optional)
- Ribbon (optional)

Choosing materials
With this project, it is a good idea to mix up the papers you use to add some depth to the design. Think about using tissue or crêpe papers to add some volume and then heavier papers and thin cardstock for the more intricately cut leaves and petals so the design is visible.

Template is on page 119

1 Cut out all the parts of template 29 on page 119. To use the templates more than once or to re-size them, photocopy or trace them, following the instructions on page 24.

2 Using invisible tape, attach one of the templates to your chosen paper. If you want to layer two or three sheets of paper to cut out several petals or leaves at the same time, secure the layers together by placing small pieces of invisible tape down the sides (see page 23).

3 Using a craft knife on a cutting mat, cut out the white parts of the template and the paper(s) at the same time. Start with the details inside each design, then cut around the outside edge with scissors. Repeat this with the other templates until you have a variety of flowers and leaves in different sizes and shapes, cut out of different weights and colors of paper. When building your flowers you want to have lots of pieces to choose from—so the more the merrier at this stage.

4 Now you can start building your hair band. Build up several flowers by layering different shapes and sizes of flower centers together with double-sided tape or adhesive. Remember you can include some tissue paper shapes in among the petals to add some volume.

Variations
- Vary the colors you use depending on the occasion. For a summertime party, use bright colors such as pink, orange, and yellow; or go for orange, black, and gold for a Halloween/ autumnal party. See pages 32–33 for more ideas.
- If you don't have a hair band, use a length of ribbon and attach the corsage project on pages 66–67 to the ribbon and wear it in your hair.
- You could also try attaching small flowers to the ends of short lengths of craft wire and wrapping the wire around the hair band to give it some height.

TAKE SPECIAL CARE
Circled in red are the trickiest areas to cut. Try to keep each small detail separate from the ones either side of it.

5 Once you have made the flowers, you need to attach them to the hair band. Place a small piece of double-sided tape (or a small amount of adhesive) on the back of each flower, remove the backing paper, and press the flower firmly onto the hair band. I find it looks better to attach the flowers slightly to one side, rather than right in the center.

6 Once you have attached the flowers, you can add a few extra petals and leaves. Slide them underneath the flowers so that the joins remain hidden.

FLOWER GIRL
Daisy colors make this hair band a great accessory for the summer months. Deeper shades of red, purple, or even gold would transform it for the festive period.

Decorate the entrance to your home with these lanterns. This project has been designed with Halloween in mind, guiding the way for trick-or-treaters and creating a spooky glow at your front door or on your window ledge.

Tool kit
- Craft knife and blades
- Cutting mat
- Invisible tape
- Double-sided tape
- Metal rule

Materials
- Paper
- Small glass or tealight holder
- Tealight candle

Choosing materials
When choosing paper for this project, think about the color you are going to use and the thickness of the paper. The thinner the paper, the more light will shine through. If the paper is a dark color, then your cut-out sections will be more visible. I like to make some lanterns with light-colored paper and some with dark, as you get different effects with each lantern.

Template is on page 95

1 Cut out or photocopy template 2 on page 95, being careful to include the small tab that runs along the right-hand edge as you will need this to construct your lantern. To create a lantern that is approximately 6 in. (15 cm) tall and will hold a regular tealight candle, re-size the template to 150%. You can do this by scanning into a computer or on a photocopier (see page 24).

2 Using a craft knife and a metal rule on a cutting mat, cut a piece of paper the same size as the template. Remember not to cut off the tab at this point. You need to leave room on your paper for this, too.

3 Using invisible tape, fix the template on top of the paper, carefully aligning the edges.

4 Before you start cutting out the design, fold the template and paper along the dotted lines on the template. Fold them in half first, then fold the two sides in on themselves again to create a box shape. Lastly, fold the thin tab at the end of the design. Use your fingers or a bone folder to firmly press down on the edges and create sharp creases.

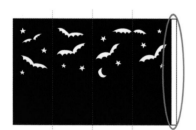

TAKE SPECIAL CARE
Remember not to cut your design too close to the edge of the paper as you must keep a tab free to fix the double-sided tape to.

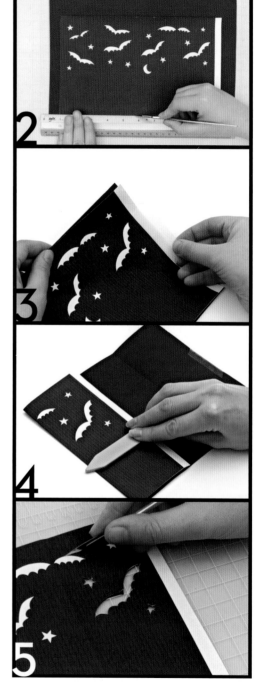

5 Open out the paper so that it is flat again. Using a craft knife on a cutting mat, cut out the white parts of the template and the paper at the same time. Be careful when cutting around the folded edges, as they can be more likely to tear.

6 Once you have cut all the white areas, remove the template and fold the paper again along the crease lines you made in step 4.

7 Place a narrow strip of double-sided tape along the tab section, peel off the backing paper, and press the tab onto the other side of the design to make the box.

8 Place a tealight candle inside a glass or candle holder, pop it inside the lantern, and watch the shadows come to life.

MOOD LIGHTING
These lanterns are a great way to add some mood lighting to your room. Watch the spooky shadows that will be cast from the lanterns dance around your room.

Safety tip
Never leave a lit flame unattended. I put the tealights in glasses inside the lanterns for safety, too.

Decorate your gifts with these paper-cut gift tags, personalizing them for each recipient by adding their initial. Co-ordinate them with the wrapping paper for a truly elegant-looking gift.

Tool kit
- Craft knife and blades
- Cutting mat
- Metal rule
- Invisible tape
- Scissors
- Sticky foam dots

Materials
- Thin cardstock in different colors
- Ribbon

Choosing materials
Any weight of paper can be used for this project, but thin cardstock works particular well, as it is strong. Co-ordinate your color choice with the rest of your wrapping to create an elegant and thoughtful gift.

Template is on page 125

TAKE SPECIAL CARE
Don't forget to cut the hole at the top of the bottom layer of your papercut so you can attach the ribbon to finish your gift tag.

1 Cut out both parts of template 38 on page 125. To use the templates more than once or to re-size it, photocopy or trace them, following the instructions on page 24.

2 Cut a piece of cardstock to fit the template. Using invisible tape, attach the template for the first layer of the gift tag to the cardstock.

3 Using a craft knife on a cutting mat, cut out the white parts of the template and the cardstock at the same time. Cut the small details within the template before cutting around the outside edge. Remove the template.

4 Repeat steps 2 and 3, using the circle template for the second layer of the gift tag and a different color of cardstock. If you used a light color for the first layer, then it might be nice to choose a darker color for this layer.

5 If you want to add an initial or initials to your gift tag, use the guide on pages 30-31 to draw or photocopy a template. Using invisible tape, attach the template to cardstock. Using a craft knife on a cutting mat, cut out the letter.

6 Place small sticky foam dots on the back of the first layer, then attach it to the center of the circle. Attach the letter to the center of the first layer in the same way.

7 Thread a length of ribbon through the hole in the second layer and attach the tag to your gift.

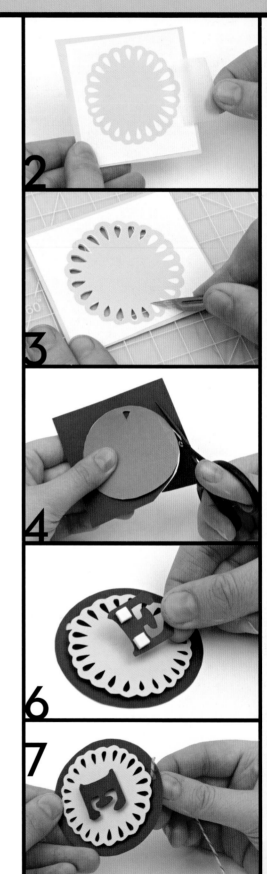

TO YOU FROM ME
Choose your shape carefully to suit the recipient and the occasion and pick colors that perfectly complement your wrapping paper choice for an irresistible gift.

After a great party, why not send your guests away with a sweet treat parceled up in these little gift bags? They would make great favor bags for weddings, too.

Tool kit
- Craft knife and blades
- Cutting mat
- Metal rule
- Invisible tape
- Bone folder
- Double-sided tape or other adhesive, such as a glue stick

Materials
- Thin cardstock
- Ribbon

Choosing materials
Use a thin cardstock rather than paper for this project as it is stronger, which means that the gift bags will hold your sweet treats better, be more durable, and can be used again.

Template is on page 127

1 Cut out template 43 on page 127. To use the template more than once or to re-size it, photocopy or trace it, following the instructions on page 24.

2 Using a craft knife and metal rule on a cutting mat, cut a piece of cardstock to fit the template. Using invisible tape, attach the template to the cardstock.

3 Using a craft knife on a cutting mat, first cut out the white details at either end of the template, cutting through the template and the cardstock at the same time. Remember to cut the little holes below the pattern (this is for the ribbon tie). If you are feeling brave, try cutting through two layers of cardstock at once to save time when making lots of gift bags (see page 23).

4 Place a metal rule on the dotted lines on the template and score along them with a bone folder. Scoring them now will make it easier to fold the bag when you remove the template.

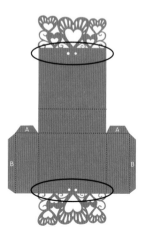

TAKE SPECIAL CARE
Circled in black are the trickiest areas to cut. Pay special attention to the areas where the cut-out element joins the bag, as overcutting here will cause the top section to be weak and break easily.

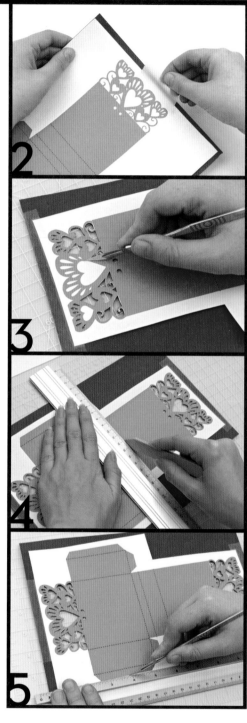

5 Using a craft knife and metal rule on a cutting mat, cut around the edge of the template. Remove the template.

6 Once the template is removed you should be able to see the score lines you made in step 4. Fold the bag along these lines, using a bone folder or your fingers to create sharp creases.

7 Attach a small piece of double-sided tape to the small tabs (marked A on the template), peel off the backing paper, fold the tabs over, and press onto the bottom panel of the bag. Repeat this with the side tabs (marked B on the template) to secure the sides of the bag in place.

8 Fill up the gift bag with some sweet treats, thread a length of ribbon through the holes at the top of the bag, and tie in a bow.

GORGEOUS GIFTS
Show your guests you care with these thoughtful and impressive party favor bags. They'll be thrilled before they've even peeked inside.

Variation
Be creative and come up with your own decorative top, so that these bags can be used for different occasions. Add some Halloween motifs for trick-or-treaters or some snowflakes to make lovely packaging for Christmas gifts.

With these drink tags, you will always know whose glass is whose at a party! They also add a decorative touch to your wine glasses. Be creative in coming up with your own designs and make them in a variety of colors so that each guest has a different one.

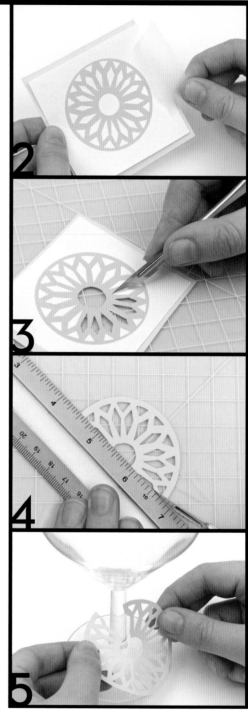

Tool kit
- Craft knife and blades
- Cutting mat
- Metal rule
- Invisible tape

Materials
- Paper or thin cardstock
- Low-tack poster putty (optional)

Choosing materials
Cardstock or paper can be used in this project, but if you would like to use the tags again then use a thin cardstock, as it is stronger and will withstand wear and tear better. You may want to laminate the tags to make them water resistant in case any little drink spillages occur.

Template is on page 131

1. Cut out template 50 on page 131. To use the template more than once or to re-size it, photocopy or trace it, following the instructions on page 24.

2. Using a craft knife and metal rule on a cutting mat, cut a piece of cardstock to fit the template. Using invisible tape, attach the template to the cardstock.

3. Using a craft knife on a cutting mat, carefully cut out the white details within the template and the center circle. Carefully cut around the edge of the template, then remove the template.

4. Now make a slit in your design so that you can attach it to a wine glass. To do this, pick a point on the outside edge of your drink tag and, using a craft knife and a metal rule, cut a straight line from the outside edge to the center circle.

5. Repeat steps 1–4 until you have enough drink tags for all your glasses. To attach each to a glass, simply lift one of the edges of your tag next to the slit and slide it onto the base of the glass. It should stay in place— but if you want to make extra certain, put a tiny bit of low-tack poster putty under the tag.

TAKE SPECIAL CARE
Don't forget to cut a slit from the outside edge to the center of the circle so you can attach the drink tag to your glass.

Variation
Try cutting less detail out of the designs and leaving a space to write each guest's name in. They know which drink is theirs and you could make multiple drink tags in the same color.

SINGLED OUT
Use a combination of colors and designs to ensure that every guest will have their own unique drink tag.

Add some paper-cut decoration to your cake display with these wrappers that can either go around your cake or around your cake stand.

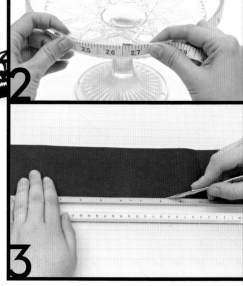

Tool kit
- Craft knife and blades
- Cutting mat
- Invisible tape
- Double-sided tape or other adhesive, such as a glue stick
- Tape measure
- Small pins

Materials
- Paper

Choosing materials
Choose a lightweight paper for this project, because you are going to have to cut through lots of layers at once; you could even use something as light as tissue paper. As the design will be attached to your cake or cake stand, it doesn't have to stand up on its own.

Template is on page 129

1 Cut out template 46 on page 129. To use the template more than once or to re-size it, photocopy or trace it, following the instructions on page 24.

2 Measure the circumference of your cake or cake stand with a tape measure.

3 Using a craft knife and metal rule on a cutting mat, cut a piece of paper that is the same height as the template, and the circumference of the cake or cake stand in length. To make the wrapper fit perfectly, you may need to re-size the template. Ideally, you need to make sure that a whole number of templates fits into the length of the paper—otherwise the edges won't match. But, you can get around this problem by having that section of wrapper at the back of the cake, so that no one can see it.

4 Using invisible tape, attach the template to one end of the paper, then accordion fold the paper behind the template (see page 23).

TAKE SPECIAL CARE
Circled in red are the trickiest areas to cut. These areas are on the fold and must stay connected. Do not cut through the folds or the wrapper will not hold together when unfolded.

Tip
It is better to round up than round down when measuring your cake and your paper. It is preferable to have a longer wrapper that overlaps slightly at the back, rather than being left with a gap.

5 Once your paper is accordion folded (inset), use a craft knife on a cutting mat to cut out the white parts of the template and the paper at the same time. As there are several layers of paper to cut through, take your time, as the stack may be quite thick.

6 Carefully cut around the edge of the template, remembering not to cut along the folded edges as the design will fall apart. Remove the template.

7 Unfold the paper to see the full design. To attach the wrapper to a cake, insert a few small pins through the wrapper into the cake. To attach it to a cake stand, stick a length of double-sided tape along the bottom of the wrapper, and attach this to the rim of the cake stand. Now your cake is ready to add to your party table.

Variation
You will find different templates on page 129 including the flower design shown right, so this project can be used for lots of different parties. Alternatively, try designing your own—just remember that your design needs to go all the way to the edge of both sides so that the folded layers have something to connect to.

LET THEM EAT CAKE
Make your baked treats look even more delectable with these cake wrappers. From spooky Halloween designs to pretty floral motifs, you can add something special to any cake-filled occasion.

This intricate birthday card is a great project to attempt once you have become confident in your papercutting, and it gives you the chance to really show off your talents. You could make a large card for a special birthday or even place this papercut in a frame to create a unique birthday gift for your loved ones!

Tool kit
- Craft knife and blades
- Cutting mat
- Metal rule
- Invisible tape
- Bone folder (optional)
- Glue stick
- Spray adhesive

Materials
- Two contrasting colors of paper—one for the paper-cut motif and one for the circle behind
- Medium cardstock for the main body of the card

Choosing materials
When choosing your paper and cardstock for this project, think about the colors that you are going to use. Choose contrasting colors for the backing card and the paper for the motif. You will need to write a message inside the card, so if you choose a dark color cardstock, you may need to use a silver or gold pen or apply an insert. The card should stand up on its own so a medium cardstock is recommended.

Template is on page 139

TAKE SPECIAL CARE
Circled in red are some areas to watch out for. There are some intricate details so don't rush, and make sure that all the areas are securely connected to each other.

1 Cut out template 55 on page 139. To use the template more than once or to resize it, photocopy or trace it, following the instructions on page 24.

2 Using a craft knife and metal rule on a cutting mat, cut a piece of paper to fit the template. Using invisible tape, attach the template to the paper.

3 Using a craft knife on a cutting mat, cut out the white parts of the template and the paper at the same time. Work systematically: start in the middle and work your way outward. This is a very intricate design, so take your time.

4 Cut around the outside edge and remove the template.

5 Measure out a square that fits around the motif, leaving plenty of room around the edge. Next, cut a rectangle from a different colored cardstock that is the same height as your measured square and double the length, creating a rectangle. This will form the main body of your card.

6 Fold the cardstock you have just cut in half carefully to create the main body of the card. Use a bone folder to create a sharp crease if you wish.

7 Place the paper-cut motif on another piece of paper in a third color and draw a circle around it. Cut out the circle and, using a glue stick, attach it to the front of the folded card, centering it carefully. It is a good idea to cut the background circle very slightly smaller than the motif so that it won't show at the edges but will still appear behind all of your cut-out areas.

8 Spray the back of the paper-cut motif with spray adhesive, leave it to become tacky, then attach it over the circle on the front of the card.

HAPPY BIRTHDAY

Take your time over your cutting and choose your colors carefully to produce a handmade birthday card with the wow factor.

7
8

PARTY TIME
Using elements from a number of projects you could throw a charming party decorated with your own papercuts.

3
TEMPLATES

Now we get to the section where you can actually begin to cut up this book! In this section you'll find 60 exciting and unique templates, that you can cut straight out of the book ready to begin your papercutting journey.

A dotted line is marked down the edge of each page to show where to cut out the template. Use a craft knife and a metal rule on a cutting mat to do this. You will notice that many of the pages have more than one template, so you might want to use a pair of scissors to cut out the individual templates as you need them, rather than removing the whole page straight away.

If you don't want to cut up this book, then you don't have to—you can trace or photocopy the templates instead. You'll find instructions for how to do this on page 24. This allows you to re-size or modify the designs and keep the original templates in the book to use again and again. Next to a few of the templates you will see a recommended percentage for you to resize the template to create the project at a particular size, as outlined in the project.

Every template is numbered so that you can easily find the right template for your project. There are more templates than projects, which gives you lots of designs and variations to choose from. Every extra template has a reference to a project that uses the same techniques, so you can follow the steps to keep you on track.

TEMPLATE 1
**Halloween
lanterns,
pages 78–79.
Enlarge by
150%.**

TEMPLATE 2
**Halloween
lanterns,
pages 78–79.
Enlarge by
150%.**

TEMPLATE 3
**Accordion-fold
invitation,
pages 38–39.**

TEMPLATE 4
**Party
garlands,
pages 46–47.**

TEMPLATE 5
**Party
garlands,
pages 46–47.**

TEMPLATE 6
**Party
garlands,
pages 46–47.**

TEMPLATE 7
Tree table decorations, pages 54–55.

TEMPLATE 8
Tree table decorations, pages 54–55.

TEMPLATE 9
**Paper wreaths,
pages 52-53.**

TEMPLATE 10
**Paper wreaths,
pages 52-53.**

TEMPLATES 11
AND 12
**Hanging
paper
rosettes,
pages 48–49.**

TEMPLATE 13
**Pop-up festive
card, pages
42–43.**

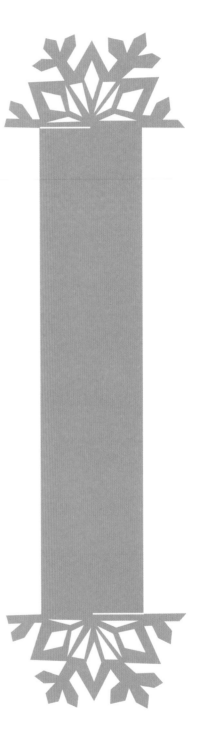

TEMPLATE 14
Napkin holders,
pages 64–65.

TEMPLATE 15
Napkin holders,
pages 64–65.

TEMPLATE 16
Napkin holders,
pages 64–65.

TEMPLATES 17, 18, AND 19
Cake toppers, pages 68–69.

TEMPLATES 20 AND 21
Cake toppers, pages 68–69.

TEMPLATE 22
**Flower corsages,
pages 66–67.**

TEMPLATE 23
**Place cards,
pages 70–71.**

TEMPLATE 24
**Place cards,
pages 70–71.**

TEMPLATE 25
**Place cards
pages 70–71.**

A

B

TEMPLATE 26
**Placemats,
pages 72–73.**

A

B

TEMPLATE 27
**Placemats,
pages 72–73.**

A

B

TEMPLATE 28
**Placemats,
pages 72–73.**

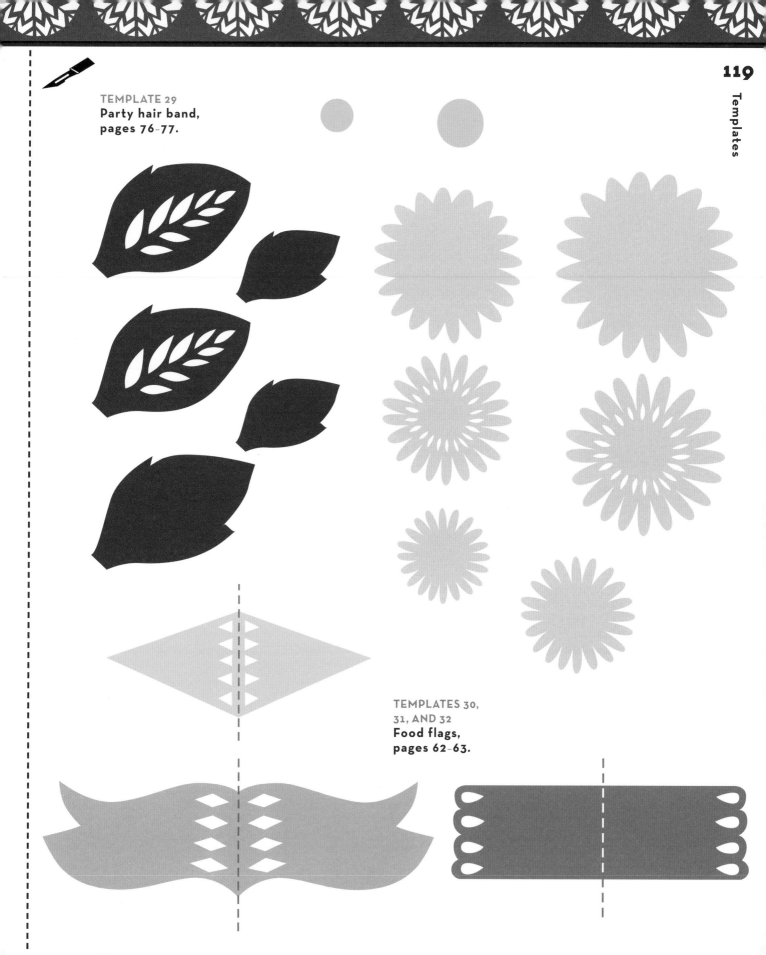

TEMPLATE 29
Party hair band,
pages 76–77.

TEMPLATES 30,
31, AND 32
Food flags,
pages 62–63.

TEMPLATE 33
**Gatefold
party
invitation,
pages
40-41.**

TEMPLATE 34
**Gatefold
party
invitation,
pages
40-41.**

TEMPLATE 35
Gatefold party invitation, pages 40–41.

TEMPLATE 36
Party pinwheels, pages 58–59.

TEMPLATE 37
Party pinwheels, pages 58–59.

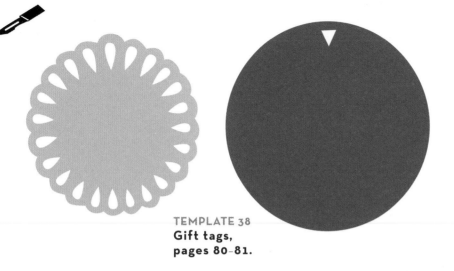

TEMPLATE 38
**Gift tags,
pages 80–81.**

TEMPLATE 40
**Gift tags,
pages 80–81.**

TEMPLATE 39
**Gift tags,
pages 80–81.**

TEMPLATE 41
**Gift tags,
pages 80–81.**

TEMPLATE 42
**Birthday buttons,
pages 74–75.**

TEMPLATE 43
**Gift and
favor bags,
pages 82–83.**

A

A

B

B

TEMPLATE 44
Cake wrapper,
pages 86–87.

TEMPLATE 45
Cake wraper,
pages 86–87.

TEMPLATE 46
Cake wrapper,
pages 86–87.

TEMPLATE 47
Patterned drink tags, pages 84–85.

TEMPLATE 48
Patterned drink tags, pages 84–85.

TEMPLATE 49
Patterned drink tags, pages 84–85.

TEMPLATE 50
Patterned drink tags, pages 84–85.

TEMPLATE 51
**Window decorations,
pages 50–51.**

TEMPLATE 52
**Window decorations,
pages 50–51.**

TEMPLATE 53
**Window decorations,
pages 50–51.**

TEMPLATE 54
**Window deorations,
pages 50–51.**

TEMPLATE 55
**Birthday card,
pages 88–89.**

TEMPLATE 56
**Dress-up props,
pages 56–57.**

TEMPLATE 57
**Dress-up props,
pages 56–57.**

TEMPLATE 58
**Dress-up props,
pages 56–57.**

TEMPLATE 59
**Dress-up props,
pages 56–57.**

TEMPLATE 60
**Dress-up props,
pages 56–57.**

Page numbers in bold type refer to templates.

All step-by-step and other images are the copyright of Quarto Publishing plc.

CREDITS

Thank you to Susan Niner Janes for creating the step-by-steps and the finished piece for the birthday card project.

This book is dedicated to our little Maggie. Keeping us on our toes from the very beginning xx